Rule of Law School

How to get through law school

Rule of Law School

How to get through
law school

DANIELA VINKELES MELCHERS

First published in 2019 by
Daniela Vinkeles Melchers

www.ruleoflawschool.com

A catalogue record for this book is available from the British Library

Images: Zdenek Sasek/Cartoon Resource, Shutterstock.com

ISBN: 978-1-9161690-9-8

For my family always,

DVM

Table of Contents

rule of law school

noun [S] **UK** /ˌruːl əv ˈlɔː/ **US** /ˌruːl əv ˈlɑː/ FORMAL

a set of rules that <u>people</u> at law school must <u>obey</u>

Preface

Once I completed my master's degree in international commercial law, I felt compelled to write this book because my studies would have been so much easier if someone had told me what to do and how to do it. This book is intended for anyone who is studying law or considering studying law, as well as for their parents. It will give you an insight into how law school works, life outside university and what happens after you have graduated. Law is one of the most challenging subjects, and it's getting tougher each year, so my aim is to counter the trend. Hopefully, I can make the process of completing your studies easier and more time efficient.

In my first class at law school, the professor said: "Look left and right – these people will not get through law school at the end of this year. You are now part of the university, and you have to start thinking like a lawyer. This means that you have full responsibility to figure out on your own how the system works." This line scared everybody, and that's exactly what the professor wanted! Fear not – it doesn't have to be this way. I will give you study tips on how to prioritise your work and save you time so that you can make the most of student life.

You might be considering going abroad during your studies, and this is also a task that requires time, energy and good preparation. I moved abroad for my master's degree to enhance my chances in the marketplace, and this experience gave me an insight into the hurdles that you also might come across. Of course, there are websites that offer advice; however, I have found that they can be unreliable and do not give a full picture of what you need to know when you are deciding to go abroad. Thus, in this book, you will find my and other students' experiences of law school, going abroad and post-university experiences.

During my study years, I noticed that most people struggle both in and after law school. Moreover, one of the most important skills you need to have for the job market is the ability to collaborate in teams and make friends. This is essential for your personal growth, regardless of the profession you end up in. Some of my friends moved abroad or took work that was way below their potential. I am talking about highly intelligent people just like you and me. It is important that you do something to complement your studies and improve your career prospects. You need to be ahead of the game. I have always worked alongside my studies so that I would be more attractive to future employers and, even more importantly, to explore my own potential. Many students choose otherwise, and they often do not stand out from the crowd when they apply for a job at a law firm, so their CVs end up in the bin. Society demands that law graduates possess legal knowledge and also the ability to demonstrate skills gained outside of their studies. Law school on its own is very theoretical, and you need to make sure that you gain life experience to complement your technical knowledge.

I was very fortunate that during the writing of my dissertation I was offered a job as a headhunter at Freshfields, which is part of the 'magic circle' of leading international law firms. I felt really honoured to receive an offer like that and chose to accept it rather than become a lawyer. My work in recruitment has given me another piece of knowledge that I want to share with you: how to secure yourself a spot in the marketplace. Having a degree does not automatically provide you with the desired job. The job market has become an insecure place – especially since the 2008 financial crisis – and the legal market is oversupplied. Hence, the competition is growing fiercely. I want to help you create more opportunities and make better choices within your chosen career path.

So why did I decide to go to law school? The short answer is that I was guided on that path by my mother. Often, your parents are the ones who know you best and can therefore tell you what your strengths and weaknesses are. My mother pushed me into law school even though I did not like to read books at all. In high school, I developed the habit of studying a few days or a day in advance for my exams and still managed to pass. That was exactly what I did for my first exam at university, and I failed! I felt so overwhelmed because it is important to start off on the right foot. The books at law school are much thicker and more complex, and the requirements of answering a question are strict because your *eye for detail and analytical mind* are being examined. Consequently, I developed the ability to read a lot, to digest the content to the essential parts and create a structured reproduction based on legal sources. I discovered a passion for books in law school, and it grew so strong that I am now writing my own book!

Rule of Law School gives you an overview of what to expect at law school and what lies ahead. You will receive a guide to the difference between studying at a common law school and a civil law school. This is crucial to know when you decide whether to go abroad and which career path potentially lays ahead of you. To optimise your opportunities, I will cover all of the important issues that most people experience during law school. I will touch briefly on how to be financially smart. The fact is, many students take a loan and will have a huge debt after studying. By sharing my knowledge with you, I hope to guide you in your pursuit of success and help you to have the time of your life during law school. This compact manual will give you an inside view of the essential parts of university life. I recommend that you firstly read this book in total and then focus on specific information for subsequent readings. Underline what is crucial to you. This is actually what you will learn at law school: where to find your sources and how to apply them.

In short, this book will tell you how to decide whether law school is for you, how to get into law school, how to master study techniques, how to make better decisions during your time at law school, and how to increase your chances of getting a spot in the marketplace.

Daniela Vinkeles Melchers

CHAPTER 1

Introduction: law school and your destiny

"The direction in which education starts a man will determine his future life."

Plato

The first Rule of Law School is: *have a positive reason for being at law school.* Do you want to become a lawyer or are you just there because you simply do not know what you want to do? If you want to become a lawyer, be prepared to work hard because it requires very long hours and learning independently. Also, if you have a clear goal in mind, you can remind yourself when things get tough. . . .!!!

The reason I chose law school was because I wanted to become a person who fights for justice, determines the rules of society and plays a significant role. I wanted to become one of the best international 'hotshot' lawyers history has ever known. By the end of law school, my reasons changed because it became clearer what law school was actually teaching me and who I wanted to become.

Law school does not only educate you to become a lawyer or a judge; it can also prepare you for other jobs such as politician, diplomat, regulator and consultant. The advantage of law school is that you can work in almost every industry! The fundamental skills you will gain are how to think systematically and how to distil relevant information. Therefore, the range of choices you have career-wise is very broad. Luckily, you do not need to choose your specialisation in your bachelor's degree.

Law school will provide you with the most common topics practised. A period of reflection after each course is essential in order to make the best decision about what you really want to do after your studies. Your path in life may change as you gain new experiences and become more aware of what is waiting for you out there. Law school can be a heavy bureaucratic process that demands a lot of time, patience and effort. Studying law will train you to think in a strategic analytical way. It will not teach you what you need to know in practice. The main lesson you receive is how to get to an analytical digested conclusion that is in line with the law. This will help you to handle and solve different types of cases according to the law and prioritise a huge workload.

The university you choose to attend is also very important, although not as important as the grades you obtain. Every university has a reputation, and it is essential to find out what that reputation is by doing your research via multiple independent media channels, or even people you might know in the business. A prestigious university can be very useful for your job applications; however, it does not necessarily deliver your dream job. You should also consider in which city you would like to live and what kind of people are attending the university. Take a look at the rankings of each university, attend open days or speak with students who actually study there.

When I was choosing my university, I got lots of advice. You have to remember that these suggestions are based on the knowledge, opinions and experiences of another person. They will not necessarily align with your preferences. You can choose to visit your top three universities to see what the atmosphere is like, and it's better to do this when there isn't an open day. In most students' experiences, open days are only a façade of the truth! They will provide you with useful information; nevertheless, the day-to-day atmosphere is lacking.

Call a friend or ask around if somebody knows a student at that university, and then join a college class and hang out there for a little while. Do not forget to ask them what days are best to visit. Fridays tend to be quieter as the weekend is approaching. By visiting, you will get a feel for whether the university is right for you; simply looking at a website will not give you the full picture. Make sure you take a look at the library because you will spend MANY hours there! If your visits are not helping you to decide whether you would like to go to law school, you could take a career test, get some professional advice and follow your instinct. You will have plenty of opportunities to change course if you do make the wrong choice.

If you have decided to make an application, you need to be aware of the second Rule of Law School: *you must be willing to work hard, develop skills and be the type of student the university is looking for.* Obviously, you need to start your reasoning here and write your first pleading. Before you start to write your application letter, you must find out what type of letter your law school wants to receive. In general, the content needs to be structured, coherent and easy to read. Don't forget, the tips I am giving you are generic – make sure you do what is required for the specific university you're applying for.

In general, application letters should be no longer than two pages. My application letter started with this famous quote from the philosopher Plato: *"The direction in which education starts a man will determine his future life."* From there, I answered the following questions: Why law? Why this university? Who am I? How will I contribute to the university? What are my ambitions after university? This is also a good exercise to explore your own mind and arguments. I searched for the best cover letters online from the best universities and used them as a template for my own letter. This allows you to follow the example of successful people who did get accepted, and it will save you time too!

In Appendix 8.1, I have added my letter of motivation to give your creative brain some ideas. Please do not copy it because universities have ways of discovering plagiarism. Being yourself is the most important ingredient!

CHAPTER 2

Theoretical: how to develop law school skills

"The starting point is to be ahead of the game."

Daniela

2.1 Preparation

Law school is all about gaining legal skills. This chapter will give you a good insight into which steps you need to take to get the best results, how to prioritise your work and having attention for detail – these are buzzwords and need to be used. There are different ways to be ahead of the game; you only need to discover what works best for you. The third Rule of Law School is: *know how to deal with a pile of books*. In other words, how to reduce a large amount of complex information in a clear, concise and coherent manner. Once you have mastered that skill, you need to know how to apply all of the knowledge obtained on paper. This can vary from exams to essays to dissertations. You need to have a positive attitude towards these tasks and be highly motivated. I will try my best to explain to you what lies ahead so you will stop procrastinating, get the work done and still have time for your family and friends.

2.1.1 Dealing with a pile of legal books

You will most likely be given a reading list at the start of your course. However, you do not necessarily have to buy all the books they recommend. Be a real lawyer and do your due diligence first to see if there are any other books that cover the topics and are shorter or easier to read. Often, they recommend you books the professor wrote himself to gain profits. Other books might be more efficient and comprehensive. In the beginning, this might take some time; however, in the long run, you will be much better off when your exam period approaches!

The first thing you should always do when you have a book in your hand is take a look at the table of contents. This is the skeleton of a book, and it allows you to quickly see what the main topics are and how they are divided into subtopics. The number of pages also gives a good indication of how much time you will need to spend on a topic.

Once you have scanned through the book, you will know whether it complies with your syllabus or course outline. So now you already know the headlines of your exams! Every question can be found within the main topic. If you do this for all of your courses, you will have an overview of what is coming. Next, you need to have in-depth knowledge of every topic. The main topics are usually divided into subtopics that give you an overview of what the details are. This can also serve as your guide for your summary, if you are making one.

Since I have studied both civil law and common law, I will touch upon both systems in section 3.3. They do overlap in terms of *how* to work within the system; nevertheless, the wording can be very different. For essay exams, there will be a range of topics you can choose from, and you need to elaborate on one topic where you can relate the various topics in a coherent manner. You can apply similar study techniques for both civil law exams and common law exams. Naturally, you need to discover what works best for you. Everyone has a different style of studying. For me, the best method to memorise and visualise the content was **mind mapping**. I digested my notes from the classes and used a textbook as an additional aid to elaborate on the content if I hadn't fully mastered the subject.

2.1.2 How to find cases and law reports

There are some research methods that work in general. The first thing I would highly recommend is to ask legal librarians for advice on how to conduct your research or if they have tours/ presentations that will help you to get the best results. Ask them when it's best to use non-electronic research and electronic research. You should go to the area of law that you need to conduct research on, and then scan all the books to see what is available and the variety of topics. Most legal libraries have catalogues or indexes where you can find all the titles. Law reports are divided into the different divisions. This is best found electronically because you can use keywords in the case law search system. Extracts and summaries of a judgement can be useful to get the case in a nutshell. However, this should not be used as a citation. You can only refer to the judgement itself. Do not forget to look at earlier cases that have been used to support the judgement. The best databases to use are LEXIS and WESTLAW. There are also journals available that cover specific areas of the law. These are, in my opinion, more useful when you need to write essays or dissertations because you can cover the most current discussions.

2.1.3 Think like a lawyer and prioritise your workload

The fourth Rule of Law School is: *see the bigger picture*. So how do you do this? At the earliest opportunity, you should write down a time schedule for your exams. Always do this as soon as possible to enhance your effectiveness. The dates should be announced by the university within the first few weeks of your course. Start with the end in mind. Analyse what needs to be done – lectures, deadlines and socials. Then take a look at a model exam. Understand where your energy and focus is going to be. Once you have seen some past exam questions, you know where you are heading. Don't worry if you don't understand everything from the start.

The main point is that you know what is required for the coming weeks and have an overview of what is expected of you. When you write your schedule, don't forget to include non-study commitments such as birthdays. This tactic will also help you to avoid procrastination. You should allow yourself to have a good time and let your brain breathe for a bit.[1] By writing down the dates, you can more easily keep an eye on how much time you have and how to best plan your social life, which is an essential part of student life! Social commitments often arise unexpectedly. In the first year of your studies, you'll be pretty much busy discovering your capabilities in terms of productivity and discipline. The following years will have less 'bumps' because you will have developed these skills and have fewer distractions.

Once you have made your schedule, you must stick to it. This requires discipline. I highly recommend distinguishing between *important* work and *urgent* work. Yes, it's urgent to do all of the reading; however, it's more important to get to the core of the

---

1   This is not an encouragement to drink!!

information. Ask the study advisers if they can provide you with a study plan or search on the internet for one, so you can learn the difference between both types of work. Ask your professor, teacher or other students about what they think is important to focus on. You will probably get some really useful tips on how to approach your pile. Collaboration during your studies is fun and enriching, and universities try to encourage it. Make sure you are around the smartest people. Making lots of friends will also benefit you in your future career because most jobs are acquired through friends.

Count the pages for each subject you need to read. Write these numbers down. Then, make sure you know how many pages you can read per hour so you can calculate how much time you need. In order to be efficient, you do not want to read every single word. Skimming is a good technique to help you quickly understand what lies ahead of you. This will help you to recognise what the professor is talking about and gain the ability to ask better and deeper questions, which builds credibility once you might actually need a favour. It will also give you a greater urge to START NOW. Believe me, the higher your grades, the higher your future pay cheque is likely to be. Let this be a motivation rather than relying on coffee.

2.1.4 Mind mapping

Equip yourself with some blank sheets of paper, a pen and different coloured markers. Look at the contents page, and you will see all of the relevant subjects. Let's use contract law as an example:[2]

Your content will have an introduction and first chapter: 'Formation of a Contract'. Put this in the centre of the paper, create a shape of choice around the text and add the chapter number (in this case, no. 1).

Next, you can create arrows going out of that shape, which will lead to the subtopics of the chapter. They will probably be Offer, Acceptance, Consideration, Form and Contractual Intention. Your mind map should now look like this:

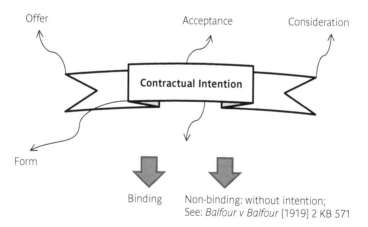

Offer

Acceptance

Consideration

Contractual Intention

Form

Binding

Non-binding: without intention;
See: *Balfour v Balfour* [1919] 2 KB 571

- First fundament
- Second rule
- Etc.

---

2 This is merely an example and does not reflect your actual contract law exam. Moreover, the skeleton is not complete – more text can be added.

This is merely an illustration to demonstrate the skeleton of the mind map. Go crazy with the shapes and colours. Your brain is programmed to visualise, and this technique is designed to break down the complexity of the work and make it more understandable. I preferred to keep one colour per sheet so my brain would tune in with the colour of the topic. Moreover, I used a different type of shape to distinguish each head topic. I stuck to the numerical order of the book to make sure the content was comprehensively and systematically programmed. Plus, it's fun to make your own 'intellectual colour drawing'. Use your notes from the tutorial to stay focused on what is expected of you.

So when I would be doing an exam and looked at the colour of the marker, I would see more than just my marker or the colour; I would see the colour that belongs to the topic. By using colour coding, you are actually building a 'memory castle' – a.k.a. *method of loci*. This technique has different styles, and a favourite of mine was to use a particular shaped arrow to lead me to a specific topic. For example, when dealing with contractual intention, I have two arrows which means that this topic is divided into two stages. Each stage possesses its own requirements that could either be established by a court case or a civil code or both. For jurisprudence or civil code, I used tabs with the same colour of that topic. When I had a question regarding contractual intention, I could already see the location within the law from a distance. This saves lots of time. In addition to exams, this system can be used during your study period. Every minute counts.

When I finished all my intellectual colour plates, I used to hang them up on my wall, make myself comfortable and then just stare at them and talk to myself. This helps you to absorb all the information and gain a better understanding of the topic. The best way to absorb information is when you are in a so-called 'alpha state' of mind.[3] Elaborate on every topic. When you don't exactly understand the wording or are not sure how to explain the topic in an analytical and comprehensive way, you can just write that topic on a separate lined blank sheet. Talk the rest of the story through, and write down **all** topics you have not mastered in detail.

Once you have finished the story, you will see that you have created a lot of complexity on just a few pieces of paper! Hoorah! Take a break, and then revise the topics you have not fully grasped. Go back to the books and study. Note down on your intellectual colour paper what you need to add, and start the whole process again. At the end when you have three courses, you will only need these digested mind maps. The fifth Rule of Law School is: *honour thy intellectual colour drawing.*

2.1.5 Model testing

I told my cousin, who is a lawyer, that my problem is not digesting the amount of texts or the complexity of the content; it was actually understanding **what** was being asked of me at exams. His response was simply: "Once you understand the question, you'll be a star." In the beginning, I didn't regard this advice as really useful because I obviously knew that I needed to understand the question – only I didn't.

To understand the question, you firstly need to know what they are aiming for and how you should structure the relevant facts in accordance with the law. When you have completed all the mind mapping, you will be familiar with all the lectures and readings.

---

3   It's a state of consciousness that heightens concentration levels according to psychic development studies.

Now, it will boil down to applying the answer to the question. How do we actually come to the point of understanding what the professors are asking of you and what they want you to cover in your answer? Studying the structure of model exam answers is the most effective way to train your brain for this task. You can get model answers from former students, study organisations and sometimes even on the university's website. If not, you have another reason to make friends and learn how to collaborate. Moreover, in classes, you will hopefully be doing exercises where you can practise the structure. Nonetheless, bear in mind that these are designed to help you understand the content of the subject and not tell you HOW to answer the actual exam questions.

Unlike the civil law system, in common law there's no such thing as 'one answer fits all'. Nevertheless, the principle of structuring a coherent answer – including directing it to the correct conclusion – still applies. In your answer, you will be reflecting on the analytical bits. Your answer must demonstrate analytical skills, and you need to learn how NOT to waste paper and words. Developing the ability to identify a legal issue and apply principles is the main reason for being at law school.

When you look at model answers, you will always see certain keywords that are relevant to the set question. You must learn to identify what is relevant and what is not. Try to outline in your mind what would make the situation change, just to understand the bigger picture. This will lead you to important elements that are not mentioned in the question, and it's always the part where you can score most points. Repeating the question is a waste of words. Memorising your mind maps will help you to analyse the situation so you can understand which direction you are going and structure your answer in the most effective way. Before the exam starts, I ask for extra paper and start writing my mind maps and have a draft that keeps the mind clear under time pressure.

For example, in a case concerning contract law and the intention of the parties during the formation, you need to elaborate on the distinction between binding and non-binding elements, as illustrated in the mind map above. However, the question could also relate to the formation of the contract. Thus, it's important to read the question carefully to understand its underlying focus.

Your answer needs to be supported with court cases and requirements or rules outlined by the court. This is not enough on its own to receive full marks. You must also APPLY your coherent explanation of the specific case and follow it with a conclusion that reflects all the crucial elements. The relevant elements are not necessarily mentioned in the question itself. You must demonstrate your legal knowledge by writing down everything that you think is significant. The emphasis is on significant, meaning stick to the question and the core of the issue. Sometimes, when you look back on your answer, you will see that there are gaps in your knowledge, so if you didn't know that a specific law was applicable, you simply need to spend more time studying.

You need to make a distinction between the ways in which a case can be applied. Your conclusion should not only consist of a summary; it must also contain the judgement according to the laws applicable. You need to be able to form a judgement upon the case according to the circumstances. Therefore, the sixth Rule of Law School is: *know how to conclude correctly in any circumstance of the case.*

Here are some examples that illustrate how you can apply analytical techniques:

EXAMPLE A

Q: A lamp has been stolen by a person under influence. Is this lawful?

Core: law and facts applied

A: Statute Stolen Lamp 2016 says *"one should not steal a lamp"* and it has been decided by the court in the case *Chair v Lamp* that this particular lamp cannot be unlawfully taken away by a person who is situated in X Y Z.

In this case, the person is situated in Y and Z. Thus, you will elaborate why this statute is applicable and what makes the act unlawful. That is where you can score marks. The lamp was taken under A B C circumstances, meaning there is no exception applicable. In casu, the court might have the authority to enforce five years of payments of [amount] because the lamp was stolen under Y and Z circumstances and this was ruled in Chair v Lamp.

Conclusion: legal consequences

To recap: the offence is covered by the Statute Stolen Lamp 2016 because this person is in situation Y and Z. This means he could be sentenced for five years of payment, since the exception is not applicable. Elaborate why the exceptions are not applicable. It is not applicable because the person was under influence. And the situation would change to seven years payment when the person was not under influence and acted in situation Y and Z. That is why I believe five years of payment is applicable under the Statute Stolen Lamp 2016 and is therefore unlawful.

NB: I hope this reflects how little information the question might contain and how much information you need to link to a certain fact. Always demonstrate the surrounding relevant facts that could be applicable that you wrote down in your mind map. Start answering in what sources you think the answer is established. Then quote the sources as much as possible. Show why this source is relevant to the question and draw a conclusion. Having a well-balanced opinion is a way of demonstrating the outcome of the law based on the facts of the question.

EXAMPLE B

Q: Alexandra got arrested without a warrant for trespassing in the UK. Is this in line with UK law?

The Criminal Law Act 1977 states:

Trespassing with a weapon of offence.

(1) A person who is on any premises as a trespasser, after having entered as such, is guilty of an offence if, without lawful authority or reasonable excuse, he has with him on the premises any weapon of offence.

(2) In subsection (1) above "weapon of offence" means any article made or adapted for use for causing injury to or incapacitating a person, or intended by the person having it with him for such use.

(3) A person guilty of an offence under this section shall be liable on summary conviction to imprisonment for a term not exceeding three months or to a fine not exceeding [level 5 on the standard scale] or to both.

(4) A constable in uniform may arrest without warrant anyone who is, or whom he, with reasonable cause, suspects to be, in the act of committing an offence under this section.

You can also just fill in the blanks *when you are short of time*:

A: Alexandra, who is on any premises as a trespasser, after having entered as such, is guilty of an offence if, without lawful authority or reasonable excuse, has with her on the premises any weapon of offence. She is intending such a use because of situation X Y and Z. Therefore she is liable on summary conviction to imprisonment for a term not exceeding three months or to a fine that does not exceed the amount of 1 million GBP. The officer in this case has therefore reasonable cause to arrest Alexandra without a warrant and handles lawfully.

NB: Please note that you must still be sure you apply the law to the facts. You should only use this strategy of answering when you are SHORT of time. It is obviously always better to illustrate cases and relate them to the facts. Be clear in your conclusion if the officer is liable so you can at least demonstrate that you understand the legal issues.

Sometimes, you need to set out several possibilities, and therefore your conclusion could also be structured as follows: *on the one hand* if the officer is in situation A, then he is liable; *on the other hand*, if he is in situation B or C then it does not show any unlawfulness to the act. Show that you understand the law even when not all facts are given to fully apply it.

In practice, your clients will only tell their side of the story, and thus some of the facts will be absent. You will become a very good lawyer when you know how to argue critically on all sides of the case. However, never make up any scenarios with no reasonable foundation as this could result in you getting points deducted.

2.1.6 Terminology types

The seventh Rule of Law School is: *make legal writing your second nature*. Legal writing is an essential skill to master. You have to develop this on your own as it is unfortunately not explicitly taught at most universities. Writing skills are often offered as supplementary courses and are not usually covered in the core law courses. However, you shouldn't really need any formal training in this area because you will absorb the terminology and writing style when you are reading. Terminology is **key** to success, and you should always use keywords in your exams and essays. The terminology can be divided into four different types.

The first terminology type is the explanation of definitions. This means defining the terms in a concise manner with specific relevant words. In law books, all chapters start with definitions. For example, the text below is from Section 1 of the UK Theft Act, which gives the basic definition of theft. I have underlined the terminology your professor wants to see in your answer.

(1) A person is guilty of **theft** if he dishonestly appropriates property belonging to another with the intention of permanently depriving the other of it; *and* "thief" and "steal" shall be construed accordingly.

(2) It is **immaterial** whether the appropriation is made with a view to gain, or is made for the thief's own benefit.

Underlining keywords is what you should do in all your books. Underline all significant keywords and learn their definitions by heart or at least know what you are talking about. It's a good idea to use different types of underlining to make distinctions. Using only one colour and no underlying system will not create a good overview and will thus not be effective. For example, I bold-lined definitions with a marker and underlined the explanations of the definitions with a pen. The elements to make definitions complete I underlined separately with a pencil.

There is a reason why law books start with definitions, so you need to start with the basics. This is fundamental to gaining an in-depth knowledge of legal issues. Definitions change over the years and are often affected by court rulings, so you need to know your jurisprudence and the social development that precipitated the change. This information can be found in your notes from lectures and books.

The second type of terminology you have to reproduce is precedents. When you are dealing with a lot of jurisprudence, try to firstly establish the theme of the case and then get to its essence. You can only do this by linking the relevant facts of the case with the relevant jurisprudence. You need to discard non-relevant information. Do so by reasoning why it is not relevant and why other facts are. Therefore, you dissect the essence of the precedent, and, in consequence, you apply the question to the case. Many students apply certain facts to their answers that are not applicable to the precedence and thus get marks deducted. Make sure you get the bigger picture by knowing the background of the precedent, the reasons given for it and the hierarchy of judgements. You will need to memorise exactly what the key determining factors are of the precedence, what the reasonings of establishment are (*ratio decidendi)* and how the reflections of the background were summarised by the court (*obiter dictum*). The question will require you to recognise the situation and apply the law to the given case. Once you possess the structure of the reasoning of the court and *apply* it to the case, you will gain a true understanding of *what* is asked of you.

The third type of terminology involves organisations. This terminology type is predominantly required in process law courses. Everything in our world is regulated by law, and law is regulated by organisations and the bodies/organs within them. Depending on which type of law you are dealing with, you will need to understand the structures of these regulatory bodies. Each part of an organisation has specific powers. It is your job to determine whether the process within that specific conduct is correctly followed by the organisation in question. In every exam, they will ask you *who* is responsible or *how* does the process work. For example, in administrative law, you can file a complaint. You need to prove in your exams that you have a full understanding of each type of complaint, which type of process it goes into and how that process is established in the law. More importantly, you need to know the exceptions! The exceptional cases dominate exam questions. Therefore, I try to illustrate that each type of law is distinct in its fundamental thinking.[4]

The fourth type of terminology is Latin. You will find a lot of Latin in legal literature. This is crucial for your essays – especially when you have an ambition to work internationally. In the international community, Latin bridges the gaps between languages. It prevents words from getting lost in translation. A history of law will give you a deeper understanding of the background to this.

One of my favourite universally recognised Latin rules is *Lex specialis, derogat lex generali*. This means that *the specific law repeals the general law*. This rule is useful to know for the application of your exam questions because it explains how to prioritise conflicting rules in a very easy way. The rest of the content they will teach you in the courses. Some teachers will tell you this is

---

4 Criminal, public and private law are distinct in their fundamentals; thus, the system of application is different.

not used anymore. Nevertheless, it's better to make sure you're a proper law student who has mastered all of the terminology. Even if you don't need this knowledge explicitly for your exams, you will need it in the international practice to distinguish yourself from the crowd. Lawyers love grammar jokes, so Latin terminology can come up in job interviews or on social occasions. You'll feel more confident if you've done your homework correctly.[5]

Finally, you should keep in mind the eighth Rule of Law School: *know the RELEVANT facts*! Without factual reasoning, you'll either apply the law incorrectly or you just won't get to the crux of the issue. This element is the main reason why students fail their exams. Understanding a legal question means understanding the relevancy of the facts; consequently, you will know which law is applicable. When you can reason in a coherent and structured manner based on the facts of the case with the applicable law, you can go from being an okay law student to an excellent one.

If you do not possess this skill, I would highly recommend that you study by mind mapping to the model answers. This allows you to examine your own analytical thinking process and correct yourself once you see how the answer should be written. The specific relevant facts will shape and support your arguments and conclusion. If you can apply the law methodically with the relevant facts, you have an incredibly useful life skill. It takes time to master this technique. Do not listen to other students when they brag and you don't get it as quickly. Everyone has their OWN learning curve, and you should ask your teachers for help with these issues because they are the ones who mark you in the end. That is a fact.

---

5   Yes really – some partners get bored and like some entertainment in their interviews. Don't underestimate the social skills needed in the industry.

2.2 Application: essays and dissertation

Now that we have covered how to prepare for your exams, it's time to apply your actual knowledge. As we know, examination styles at each university can vary. When the questions require exact answers, you can just follow the model answers. When you need to prepare for essay-style examination questions, you can still find this chapter useful. However, this chapter will mainly cover writing essays as homework and a dissertation in generic terms – where to start, how to avoid information overload, how to conquer procrastination (we all kind of love it), how to deal with bureaucracy, and brilliant minds who do not know how to teach.

Essays and the dissertation do have some differences. In general, an essay is a short piece of writing that is divided into paragraphs and has a conclusion at the end. Obviously, the dissertation is way longer and a much tougher process to go through. Yes – size does matter. Secondly, for an essay the topics are given, while for a dissertation you may choose a topic of interest. Thirdly, the dissertation will reflect your academic writing skills and how you have mastered the scholarly methods. It will be expected that you know how to create a comprehensive discussion. However, while essays and dissertations have their differences, the technical tips I will give you in this chapter can be applied to both.

Lastly, there are two types of students: the ones who buy their essays and dissertation and the ones who actually write them. I encourage you to write everything yourself because it's a skill you will have for life; plus, you will actually deserve your diploma![6] This chapter will help you to become an academic writer.

---

6   Yes, it is a form of cheating because you did not write it and pretend you did. This is also a warning to parents to be aware of the academic performance of your child. We students do need support and motivation sometimes, even though we are adults.

2.2.1 Writing THE piece: choosing a topic

Firstly, you will need to set yourself a deadline for making a decision on which topic to choose. When you fail to do this, you can become indecisive and will lose time. I would recommend spending 10% of the given timeframe on this. For example, when you're given a month to write your essay, you have three days to do your research and understand what motivates you to choose the topic. You might be drawn to a topic because it truly interests you and you would like to pursue a career in that field or because of its simplicity or complexity.

When you conduct research, make bullet points for each topic you want to cover. These can be keywords that should be covered in your master piece and will outline the spectrums of the topic you might want to discuss. This will help you understand the topic better and identify controversial subtopics and key arguments. Once you have a list, mark the ones you think are relevant enough to devote a whole chapter or paragraph to. Then check the amount of information about the topic that is available. The topic with up-to-date information that is diverse and contradictory is the one that will stand out. Often, this will show what actually interests you or what the easiest topic is to write on. Topics that are not covered too much in literature can be key for someone who wants to pursue an academic career. This could be your first research that actually gains recognition in the field you are working in. Nevertheless, how far you reach depends very much on who your mentor is. Most mentors do not really know what to do; thus, it is good to have a second contact in the academic world who can function as your sounding board.

Next, skim the text. Do not go into intensive reading at this stage, as it will take too much of your time, and you will end up suffering from a lack of sleep and being overwhelmed by the amount of notes you have. Do this in less than two days if a month has been given. You will see the bigger picture of what needs to be covered in your essay. When you have discovered what interests you and what doesn't, you can start crossing off a few of the given topics. Within the remaining time, you'll need to focus on getting your key arguments on paper. The best topics are the ones that are controversial, recently amended within their ruling or possess a wide interpretation scope in the industry, country or practice.

Lastly, with the keywords, you will now analyse what arguments you can find to point out the contrast of the problem. Readers do not want you to summarise texts or be too descriptive. They want you to be able to argue on both sides of the coin. The ninth Rule of Law School is: *no matter how thin the coin is, it always has two sides.* Look into different types of arguments you can apply, such as questioning, theories, problem solving and solution thinking, challenging and contrast argumentation. This will reflect your cognitive thinking process and how diverse it can be. To shine in the critical thinking aspect, the background and factual research you conduct needs to be systematic and strategic. If you do not limit yourself, you can get overwhelmed and lose too much time in processing all the material. Once you have your argumentation, start elaborating with supportive points.

Your reader will ask very simple questions starting with why, how, what, etc. This serves to probe your clarity, truthfulness and ability to think outside the box. The more creative you are, the better. So, do not drown yourself in the books. They are merely a support to enhance your knowledge. You have (hopefully) a good brain that possesses common sense, and you can make the case livelier as if you're actually the judge who needs to decide which side to choose.

Where do you start with choosing a dissertation topic? The tenth Rule of Law School is: *start with the end in mind.* What do you want to become and what interests you? I always thought I was going to be an international lawyer and had an interest in the BP oil spill in the Gulf of Mexico, which was big news at the time. My personal interests were leaning more to aspects of private law such as tort law and contract law. I chose damages as the topic for my dissertation. I was interested in questions like 'How are they going to pay for it?' and 'How will this be determined?' Thus, I wrote my bachelor's thesis on International Oil Pollution Damages.

For my master's dissertation topic I was looking at the development of the legal world. I saw that there were many conventions that kept on being rewritten, even when some of them could have been based on 'common sense' in the early days. I was interested in probing why certain regulations were not established. The conventions themselves did not really excite me as that involved comparing loads of deficits and arguing why certain developments were positive. The crux of the point is developing 'commercial awareness' – meaning what actually happens in practice and the background of choices made by the industry to keep the conduct in practice. You need to understand at the end of your studies that the world is affected by what we write, adopt and implement. This is also one of the key skills you need to possess as a lawyer. Consequently, you will see the 'bigger picture'.

Thus, follow the news and discover what topic or industry fascinates you – it will really give you the feeling you can add value to that particular subject. You will need to look for the legal relevance of the topic and then check the availability of sources. The quality of these sources is crucial because most academic readers will focus primarily on your bibliography. The eleventh Rule of Law School is: *the bibliography must reflect your understanding of how to conduct academic research.*

What to do now:

- Reflect on what you have learned so far during your studies and what caught your interest the most. Know what you are good at or want to become better at.

- Think about what you would like to do within your career. This does not have to be the determination of the direction of your life; it is merely an exploration of what you want so that you have something to build upon. The subject you are writing on could also function as a supporting argument for future applications to employers.

- What have you been following in the news that is fascinating to you and has a legal cornerstone? This can also be a good start to decide what type of industry catches your attention.

- Compile a top-three shortlist and summarise your topic based on the sources available, the type of arguments you can come up with, and questions that will help you to draw a conclusion.

- Book an appointment with your supervisor and ask other students what they think.

- If you are not keen on talking to other people about your topic, simply look for other equivalent dissertations that have been published by recognised universities. They might help to inspire you and function as a good stepping stone for your research and structure.

2.2.2 Writing your draft statement

Once you have found a field of interest within the law and matched that with the topic, you will quickly get to the crux of the statement. It is important to formulate your statement in a specific rather than abstract way that clearly sets out the purpose of the thesis. It needs to be clear what side you will be arguing for and the position you are presenting. You can take a normative point of view where you will support or justify that a certain statement, rule or result is beneficial to society, the economy, institutions or any other realm you could possibly think of. Are you writing in favour or will you contradict the topic?

Example:[7] You are doing or pursuing a master's in international criminal law. Which topic do you enjoy writing or reading about most? How does that topic fit in current affairs? Is there a current topic that you would like to address? A possible thought process structure:

- I enjoyed reading or writing about crimes against humanity: a topic.
- I am interested in ISIS *v.* the Anonymous group: a subtopic.
- I am interested in the procedural issues and conventions: an issue in the subtopic.
- I am interested in the law of evidence – especially the standard proof for judgement v. the burden of proof within cybercrime: your focus shifted to a specific principle in law within a broad topic. This shows that you are avoiding any general terminology and abstractions.

Therefore, you can write something about the procedural law related to the crimes against humanity that the Anonymous group is justifying with its breaches of cybercrime. Your statement needs to be as specific as possible. This will keep you better focused when writing your piece.

---

7   I am not a specialist in international criminal law – this example merely demonstrates the thinking process you should have in order to help you formulate your dissertation statement.

Now you have a feel for how to get to your statement. Consider who your audience will be and produce arguments that will lead to solving a problem. Once you know the amount of arguments, sources etc., you can make a good estimation of the worthiness of your statement and your motivation in writing about it. Start drafting a proposal for your professor. Bear in mind you need to allow time for reanalysing your data. Hardly anyone gets it right the first time. If you do: bravo! If not, do not feel guilty about taking a break. Sometimes, when you go out and discuss it with your friends, you might discover new ideas that can help you through the process. Or you can receive a revelation out of the blue. The latter works the best in my opinion because you are not tense and tend to have more creative sparks.

It is best to include an approach section, with a hypothesis and an overview of what topics you would like to cover. The best way to present your statement is to have a title and a short introduction or an abstract of the arguments plus the bibliography. The abstract/introduction needs to be based on the primary sources you would like to emphasise. Follow a professor or someone who is recognised as an authority on the subject. Write down some questions that will lead you to the solution or the direction you would like to be heading. You probably won't know what the exact solution is at this point. Nevertheless, you will need to present two sides of the coin to keep your topic interesting. The answer could be interpreted in different ways, or you might have found a discrepancy. You are being trained to become a lawyer, so make sure your audience knows what you will be addressing, which side you will represent and the reasons why.

2.2.3 Structuring your writing

Most universities will provide you with a guideline of the format required. This will include how many words, your front cover details, methodology and due date. The most basic structure is:

- Front page with university requirement details
- Abstract
- Table of contents
- Introduction
- Body
- Conclusion
- Bibliography
- Appendices

I recommend you keep it simple and devote most of your time developing the content. As mentioned before, the introduction will outline what will be discussed, the reasons/purpose/background of the dissertation and what the problem is you would like to solve.

In the body, you will present a layered structure of topics that need to be addressed to draw a conclusion. This will be your framework. Some students prefer to start with the conclusion in mind. The caveat of this method is that you will dismiss another type of conclusion. When you do choose this approach, make sure you allow yourself room to make amendments whilst developing your dissertation. It could be possible that the substance of your conclusion will change.

The arguments can have different dimensions and use different interpretation methods. Start with a hypothesis, and then evaluate each element under a different light. Consequently, it is always good to highlight inconsistencies or caveats you have found in literature, practice or results. To support your thinking, probe jurisprudential approaches, decisions, laws and regulations. After writing down your comprehensive analysis, you will have to make sure the reader understands the point you are trying to make and why your point is relevant. Make your case clear by giving direction towards your statement or standpoint. Try to take a layered structure approach, so that each chapter complies with the next and has a form of simultaneous problem-solving. The better you are at putting the puzzle together piece by piece, the better your writing will be.

The best way to create an interesting discussion is when you have opposing views. You can use concepts of philosophical thinkers such as John Locke, Thomas Hobbes, Jean-Jacques Rousseau and John Austin. This is the easiest approach in my opinion because the literature already points out the controversial thinking. All you have to do is apply their thinking and balance the debate to, for example, the regulations of laws, vagueness of concepts, the establishment of jurisprudence and its morality and so on. When I was taking a philosophical law course, I studied the debate between the scholars Hart and Dworkin. This was the perfect example of making a distinction between interpretations of law and the model of rules. These scholars are always good to use within your dissertation regardless of your subject. They developed the interpretation methods for you, so the only thing you need to do is apply them. Thus, if there are any scholars you find interesting, use their ideas to address the arguments in a different light and define their theories and positions.

Along the way, make sure you refer to the sources. This should become second nature and is crucial for your academic foundation. I cannot stress the importance of citing enough. The twelfth Rule of Law School is: *cite **all** sources in footnotes*.[8] When the

8   I will not devote time on how to cite sources as there is lots of information on this
    subject and there are different styles.

reference is not given, it will be counted as a statement without academic foundation or plagiarism, even when it might be unintentional.[9] Your university will guide you on which citation types you can choose for your footnotes. The most common reference type is the Harvard style. There are many guidelines you can use. Make sure the style you're using is actually correct. Verify this with your reader. In the end, all your footnotes will be summarised in the bibliography. Look at other dissertations to get a good idea of what a good bibliography looks like. This is actually the main point that your reader will be judging you upon. In the academic world, the sources of the research are key.

In your conclusion, you should not merely make a summary. That is simply not sufficient. This is a mistake many students make. You must reflect on the points you were trying to make throughout the dissertation. It should be more of a distillation of what you are trying to say, which is then applied to produce a solution. You should form an opinion that reflects the implication of your writing and concluding statements. Never mention anything NEW if you have not covered it in the main body. Just mention the implications of the discussion and what you suggest when you are redefining the arguments. The easiest way is to structure your conclusion as a gradual synthesis of your findings: you start off with the broader implications and context, and then slowly build to the specific or main problems or observations that support your opinion. If you can do this successfully, you can gain some recognition within the relevant industry.

9 Something you will also learn during your criminal law classes.

2.3 Presentations of justice

Some classes require you to make a presentation. There are two types of presentations: one is excellent and fun; the other is boring and sucks the life out of you.

To score high, you obviously need to deliver the first type. Besides, it is a skill necessary in business and that makes it even more important that you practice your part, so you will know what to say and project confidence. When you get nervous, just transform this energy into enthusiasm. Often, how things are said is more powerful than what you say.

It is okay to be nervous – just embrace it and take a deep breath. Albert Einstein said: *'If you can't explain it simply, you don't understand it well enough.'* You need to think about developing your skills. Even though you might not get an official grade, it is important to perform well. Your classmates might be your colleagues later, and they will remember your presentations and how well you did. Therefore, the thirteenth Rule of Law School is: *score high, even when the expectations are low.*

You will score when you . . .

- Provide a handout (not with all information) so your audience can follow the presentation and keep it for later. See this as your business card.
- Smile, introduce yourself or your team and use an icebreaker.
- Have a well-outlined structure, introduce the topics and clarify the objective.
- Keep it simple and concentrate on the core message you would like to deliver.
- Hit the crux at the start and then elaborate.
- Pose questions to the audience – raising hands makes people more engaged.

- Have a confident tone of voice and a pleasant manner. Watch your body language.
- Save your pauses for when you click to the next slide.
- Ask if there are questions when you are finished – if there are none, make sure you have a question you can answer yourself. This tactic will make you look amazing!

Do not . . .

- Read the exact words on your presentation software sheets. It will not engage the audience.
- Have a boring tone of voice!!
- Sit down, fiddle with your hands/papers or walk around too much.
- Uhm . . . uuhhh too much – know what you plan to talk about!
- Use PowerPoint – it is boring. Try Prezi, PowToon or use other interesting presentation software.
- Try to answer a question to which you do not know the answer. It is okay if you don't know all the answers. What you could do is turn to the teacher and give them the platform to elaborate when it is crucial for the class to cover this subject. This could improve your credibility.

2.4 How to deal with biased professors or feedback

Sometimes, the grade that you receive is dependent on your professor or lecturer. One of my friends told me about a lecturer who awarded high grades even when students weren't performing to a high standard. Other students were upset because their lecturer for the same course was tougher or it was impossible to achieve the same grade with the same performances and thus felt unfairly treated. Although the matter is merely dependent on the distribution of the classes, all teaching should be handled fairly.

You are entitled to raise an objection if you feel that you have been treated unfairly. This needs courage, tact and diplomacy. Since you have chosen to study law, solving problems is exactly what you will be doing in your future career.

Universities are very bureaucratic; however, so is life. Think carefully about how best to raise an issue. Most people do not like direct confrontation, and it might be worth talking to one of the student unions that actively involve themselves in these matters. Consequently, the issue will be addressed in a more tactful way. Writing an open letter to the university can also be a way of establishing some reforms. Nevertheless, the university will always be in a stronger position because departments usually have autonomy and it is very hard to scrutinise their practices. In short, choose your battles wisely – think carefully about whether this is a battle you will win and if it is worth your energy.

CHAPTER 3

Practical: get yourself ready

3.1 Going abroad

The fourteenth Rule of Law School is: *go abroad*! This requires more preparation than you think. However, it will be one of the best experiences of your life, and I would definitely recommend that you consider it. Not only will you discover a new country; you will also make new friends and get to know yourself better – especially in terms of what you would like to do career-wise. Also, you will touch upon different styles of education, gain new language skills and immerse yourself in a new culture that can enhance or contribute to your future career opportunities.

Contact your university to see what kind of study abroad pro-grammes they are connected to where you can obtain your academic goals. These programmes are often offered by the university as part of the curriculum, such as the Erasmus pro-gramme. Most universities have a website dedicated to exchange programmes and partner institutions. If you wish to go for a shorter period of time, there are interesting programmes avail-able during the summer, which are often self-funded and will give you an additional certificate. If you do not have the chance to travel in your bachelor years, you can always obtain a master's abroad. Either way, use these programmes to gain life experience because in your student years you're not restricted by a mortgage, family, job etc. Take a look at your possibilities – it's a way to learn and have fun at the same time!

3.1.1 Research, orientate and explore your possibilities

Don't know where to go? The world is your oyster, and your choice depends on what you would like to gain from the experience. If it is prestige you are looking for, then take a look at one of the university ranking sites. I recommend http://www.topuniversities.com/student-info/studying-abroad where you can find the universities subdivided into categories. They provide you with a summary of the university, statistics and a link to the website. If you have any doubts, do post something on their forum so that people who have actually experienced the university can connect with you.

If you are just looking for a cool country to go to, you simply need to work out the requirements of the university and go! You need to consider the culture, the study environment, the social lifestyle and of course the costs. For law, it's good to go to a country that has an established practice in your specialisation and professors who are reputable. This will narrow down the choices you have. Moreover, do look at the language of the course, as it might not be delivered in the language you assume.

I wanted to gain experience abroad, and I wanted to do it properly, so I went overseas for my master's. I decided to study maritime law and asked the professors at the University of Amsterdam for advice. Based on my circumstances, they recommended the UK, the US and China. It was important to me that I stay close to family and friends, so I chose the UK.

Next, I had to decide which university in the UK would be the most suitable. The prices and locations of the courses also varied greatly. I wanted to have the experience of living in London, so I narrowed it down to that region. After compiling a list of the best universities listed for maritime law in the heart of London, I booked a trip to visit some of them. Luckily, I had a friend who had the time to show me around so I could get a feel for the environment. I looked at the university buildings, the transport links, the people and what professors were available, and eventually picked a postgraduate course at City, University of London.

In the end, the choice you make is dependent on your particular needs, and hopefully you'll have a memorable experience wherever you go. It will make you look good on the national or international job market, as many businesses value international experience highly.

If you would like to stay and work in the same country after your studies, it's important to research in advance what your career possibilities are. In the Netherlands, you can apply for a training contract when you do your Master of Laws. On the contrary, in the UK you have to apply for the GDL, LPC or BPTC[10] in order to do your training contract. The UK makes a distinction between types of lawyers you can become; you can either work as a solicitor or as a barrister. The two are very different. Thus, make sure you understand your career development in advance. This will also save you money in the long term because a law degree is jurisdictional bounded. The fifteenth Rule of Law School is: *do your due diligence carefully.*

---

10 GDL: Graduate Diploma in Law; LPC: Legal Practice Course; and BPTC: Bar Professional Training Course.

3.1.2 Apply, submit and get accepted

Most universities require an application letter, which will usually need to be one or two pages long. The sixteenth Rule of Law School is: *make sure you distinguish yourself from other applicants*. This is established by an intelligent and efficient writing style. Do not construct overcomplicated sentences – they will just bore the reader! You need to use 'action words'. To inspire you, my favourites are:

Achieved	Effected	Generated	Led	Performed
Adapted	Encouraged	Guided	Listened	Persuaded
Anticipated	Established	Helped	Maintained	Planned
Assessed	Evaluated	Hosted	Managed	Provided
Built	Examined	Identified	Maximised	Presented
Continued	Executed	Illustrated	Mastered	Produced
Coordinated	Expanded	Implemented	Motivated	Questioned
Decided	Experienced	Improved	Named	Raised
Delegated	Explored	Increased	Negotiated	Recommended
Delivered	Facilitated	Initiated	Observed	Selected
Demonstrated	Focused	Interpreted	Obtained	Solved
Developed	Formed	Interviewed	Organised	Tutored
Educated	Founded	Judged	Outlined	Wrote

Your grades are obviously a major factor in the admissions process, and universities will look at the whole package, including any relevant experience and qualities. All universities have policies regarding the types of candidates they would like to attract or encourage, such as backgrounds that are under-represented. The university's website should outline the qualities required for a successful application.

Some websites are not very professional or will leave their page subject to changes. If that is the case, you can write an email to the relevant person. In this email, you should introduce yourself and ask questions with enthusiasm. They will remember you when you arrive at the university and could be your first contact point. Make a list of all the reasons why you are a suitable candidate and then reduce that down to a top five which can be used to construct a story. Deliver a pitch where you come across as a motivated student who is organised, performs at a high level and is focused on a future international career. Remember to use action words to make yourself appealing to the reader.

Make sure you plan the application process carefully. Write down all requirements, deadlines and passwords on a spreadsheet. In addition to the submission date, you should also consider any additional exams you need to take in advance for your application. For example, if you're a student from a non-English-speaking country and want to study in an English-speaking country, you will probably need to take an IELTS or TOEFL exam. Moreover, visa application processes can be daunting. Therefore, plan well in advance so that you can cover all bases. Ideally, you will submit your application a week before the deadline to make a good impression, and you will hopefully not fall into a lottery application.

Alongside your motivation letter, you will probably need to fill in other forms as well. Download these from the websites and scan through what information you need to provide. In the application form, you will usually be asked general information. Be careful with the health forms and insurances, if applicable. Do take a look at special overseas insurance policies because they can save you lots of money, depending on your insurance company and nationality.

Most universities have a 'study abroad' department. Ask them to review your application because they will know in detail what a successful application needs to contain. I will discuss how to make your CV stand out later on. Once you have received your reply, make sure all the relevant information is given. You need to know when you start, what courses you will be taking and what books are required.

In summary:

- **Step 1**

  Choose the top five foreign law schools you want to apply for and make a spreadsheet with all the dates and requirements.

- **Step 2**

  Fill in the application forms and get them checked by the departments that deal with foreign students. Outline all your educational objectives and specify your reason for choosing that country (include something about the legal system of the country concerned), university, course and experience. Demonstrate that you are an eligible, talented and enthusiastic candidate.

- **Step 3**

  Submit your application at least a week or two before the closing date so you will come across as organised and a top performer. Once it has been submitted and accepted, make sure you know who your main contact person is so you can follow up on your application. Introduce yourself and make sure you have all of the necessary information. Online, you can find many motivation letters that will give you some inspiration.

Some points you could include in your application:

- Cross-border experience that will enhance your comparative perspective.
- Studying abroad will help you to adapt to new systems.
- The course topics relate to your chosen career path.
- Refer to related high grades or experience you already obtained.
- You are looking forward to making new friends, exploring the country and learning the language – all of which will help your future career.
- You are a responsible, organised person. Give specific examples that are relevant to the course. Match your skill set with academic reasons.
- You have organised your finances to facilitate studying abroad. Give details about how you will fund your education.

3.2 Funding or no funding?

If funding is available then you must try to get some – that's a no-brainer! It's always worth trying to get some form of funding because why would you not want to save money?! This means more money for other stuff. Financial help might be available from the university or other private and public sources. The seventeenth Rule of Law School is: *write to at least five organisations that might help to fund your education.*

You can find funds through different channels. The Netherlands has a national funding book. This contains a list of *all* funds in the country subdivided by cause. Try to find a book like this in your country of choice – if it doesn't have one, you can always do research on the web or just ask the law school's relevant department if it has a list with all the relevant funds. If you feel this will take too much of your time, just pick the five funds that are most likely to accept your application. Do understand the differences between scholarships and grants. Read through their requirements, and be aware that some of them function as a loan with or without interest.

On websites like http://www.topuniversities.com/ you can find law scholarships from around the world. This website is really useful to see all funds organised per country, including a short description and a link to the relevant website. Make sure you qualify for the financial assistance. For example, the Freshfields Scholarship, in partnership with University College London, provides an interesting scheme where you will be guaranteed to receive a training contract interview.[11] For other external funding, a useful website is http://www.ukcisa.org.uk/. This provides information and advice for international students who would like to study in the UK. Try to consult only websites that have a form of authority. You can find on the bottom of this page the logo of the government's Department for Education. These types of institutions are good to ask where to find applicable grants, scholarships or any other form of funding. Just do very thorough research, make a list and state all the deadlines and requirements in an Excel sheet to keep yourself organised and less overwhelmed by the amount of funding that is available. Going through a university programme is the easiest route because it is often included within your curriculum.

---

11 See the website of UCL at the undergraduate page for funding and scholarships of Freshfields: https://www.laws.ucl.ac.uk/

3.3 Civil law v. common law

The difference between civil law and common law is also one of the factors you need to consider when you want to go abroad. In general terms, common law is uncodified, while civil law is codified. The two systems require different approaches because the exams vary between the legal systems. Studying different systems will broaden your intellect, approach and perspective. This diversity argument can also be used for your applications. I would recommend that you study both systems if the opportunity allows you – even if it's only for one semester. Having a basic understanding of the opposing legal system will help you in your career and benefit your firm or department. This is also crucial if you are planning to become a lawyer who works cross-border and deals with cases that are multi-jurisdictional.

Moreover, the way you do research will be expanded. In my experience, civil law is very much knowing and working with laws and jurisprudence, whereas with common law you have to know the background and understand the developments of society. Both are organic processes and have their advantages and disadvantages. Studying both systems will be particularly beneficial if you want to pursue an international career. The eighteenth Rule of Law School is: *get both civil and common law study experiences.*

CHAPTER 4

Putting your theory into practice

4.1 Gaining experience during law school

Studying is not enough on its own to secure yourself a position in the job market – you need to have other experiences while you are at law school. This of course also includes having fun! In addition to my studies, I did a variety of things, including signing up with a student recruitment agency and regularly working for them when they had work placements for a week or two. This is a very easy way to create opportunities. The nineteenth Rule of Law School is: *you need experience with a reputable firm or institution on your CV.*

This is an easy way to get to know the business world. To become a lawyer, you need to understand the different types of employer in terms of culture, type of work and clients. You can meet them at law fairs, where you have a chance to ask them direct questions. When I worked at Freshfields, my colleagues were always surprised about how few quality questions they received regarding the firm. Before attending a law fair, make sure you know the top three firms you would like to make an impression on, and do your homework so you actually know the differences between the law firms and certain practices. Ask the people at the stand intellectual questions. Do not just ask what it's like to work there because employees will not be objective. On the contrary, recruiters are sales-orientated. They are there to show you the benefits, so you have to read between the lines and discover the true picture yourself.

If you do not know what you would like to practise later, you could ask, for example, about the possibilities of moving between the competition law and employment law departments. Or you could ask what type of candidates the firm is looking for. Show the recruiters your CV, and ask them how it could be improved or whether anything on it interests them. I discuss other questions you could ask the recruiter in section 4.3. Taking these kinds of initiatives will make a very good impression. At the end of the conversation, remember to ask if they have a business card and if you can stay in touch. The next day, you can send a nice email to the recruiter to reiterate the meeting without mistakes!

Law firms also offer amazing programmes where you can actually be a lawyer for a day or a few days. This can be in the form of a placement scheme or a moot court. I participated in a two-day course on mergers and acquisitions at Allen & Overy, which is not taught in law school – even though it is actually a large part of commercial business. These types of programmes will give you a feel for the practice. Access was provided after a competitive application process. Hence, you will be able to meet top-notch students, showcase your intellectual talents and get to know the lawyers and partners. It's a great opportunity to gain a better understanding of a potential employer. The recruiter at the training will be judging your performance, and making a good impression will put you in a strong position to land a training contract.

Another way to have fun and gain experience is to participate at moot courts. Some universities offer really good moot court and advocacy programmes. Some of the programmes are internal, and thus you can only participate when you are part of the university. This is something that potential law school candidates should consider because it is an extra benefit your university can offer. At Oxford University, students can actually participate in moot court programmes that are connected to law firms. These are a great opportunity to get noticed by potential employers. Oxford also offers programmes for non-students. Take a look at their website for more information.

Being a part of the law society at your university is a must! You will get to know the people outside of your class, and they will become your friends. Law societies often organise trips, committees and socials. Sign up! This is very important for your CV too because it shows you're proactive and a team player – especially when you join a board.

I was also a law teacher for short courses before exams. This experience gave me a deeper understanding of the law itself and where students often make mistakes in their thinking. Unfortunately, this experience is not really valued by recruiters of law firms. However, it can be an invaluable experience if you're looking to become a professor at a university or a designer of training programmes.

Last but not least is the Model United Nations programme, where you can role play as a delegate to the UN and simulate UN committees. You will actually simulate what the United Nations does with people around the world. They are intellectually challenging because you need to understand the subject of the committee and develop a commercial and political awareness of the world. Your skills will be enhanced in negotiations, public speaking, collaborating and understanding the bigger picture, which will be your resolution. Once the work is done, you will have amazing parties where you will get to know people from all around the world. These organisations offer board or committee positions. After I participated at UNISCA, I was asked to join the board, which I did. I learned so many things from this experience, and it was great to be able to gain these skills during my student years, rather than have to learn on the job once I started work. The boards will give you a good feel for how politics works, and it is beneficial to understand this mechanical interaction before you start working at law firms. It will also enhance your career possibilities greatly. This type of experience is valued by non-governmental and governmental organisations because you will have demonstrated an interest in their type of work and you will know how to lobby.

There are many more interesting organisations or types of experiences you can gain. Just decide what suits your interests and discover what is out there. Any form of participation will add experience to your CV, help you to make new friends and learn skills you will need in the business world. Therefore, the twentieth Rule of Law School is: *sign up with organisations to gain new experiences.*

4.2 Post university

Students who graduate without any type of experience will often not be considered by prestigious employers. It's essential that you start thinking about what you want to do after law school. Once you have made a decision, you need to find out what steps you need to take in order to land your desired job. The twenty-first Rule of Law School is: *your diploma is **NOT** a guarantee you will get the job you want.* You don't necessarily have to become a lawyer after attending law school – there are many other career possibilities.

Recruiters at international law firms, such as Freshfields and Linklaters, sometimes source over 100 CVs on one single day, depending on the number of roles they have to fill.[12] Every law firm has its own requirements, so tips are provided as general guidelines for how you should be thinking when you're applying for jobs. Each law firm has its own graduate recruitment website that precisely explains what they are looking for.

The first thing you need to do is the twenty-second Rule of Law School: *get good grades*! You can have amazing work experience; however, if you do not have the grades, you will not be accepted. This will demonstrate the intellectual ability that is required. Even if you are not an all-star top student, at least have good grades for the courses you will potentially want to practise in. For example, if you are interested in private law, make sure you have amazing grades in tort, contract, property law, etc. This can also help during interviews, as you can say you are good at what interests you! This shows dedication, and it gives you an answer to the question: 'What is your weakness?' You can simply respond: 'If I am not really interested in a subject, I do not shine like a star as much as when the topic fascinates me. And private practice just fascinates me.' This can be tricky but get a feel for what sounds authentic to you.

4.2.1 What are the options on the job market?

Lawyer, judge, politician, consultant, banker, academic and entrepreneur are just some of the career paths available to law graduates. However, you are not limited to these roles. The twenty-third Rule of Law School is: *there are many more professions you can enter with a law degree besides law.* Here are some details of the roles mentioned above:

12 This figure is applicable to big cities such as London, New York and Hong Kong.

4.2.1.1 LAWYER

> *'If there were no bad people, there would be no good lawyers.'*
>
> *– Charles Dickens*

This quote is not completely true. Sometimes people act without knowledge and not necessarily with bad intention. As a lawyer, you are someone who possesses knowledge regarding a certain area. You will become a specialist in a field, or you will be a lawyer who knows bits and pieces. It all depends on the type of firm you will be working for. I will describe the types of law firms later on in section 4.3. You can also go in-house and will have a different way of working because you will be just working with one client and do all the work and not have billable hours.

Generally speaking, a lawyer gives legal advice. This means you will meet your clients, do research on the matter, draft legal documents, negotiate on necessary fronts and represent your client. You need to have commercial awareness to make sure you work within a certain timeframe and still deliver the work required. When you work at a smaller firm, you tend to be more a general lawyer who will take on cases of several areas, and you will have more client contact. When you work for a large or medium-sized firm, your work is more specialised and your tasks are often limited because of the spread. How the spread is divided is dependent on the culture of the firm.

4.2.1.2 JUDGE

> *'Injustice anywhere is a threat to justice everywhere.'*
> *– Martin Luther King Jr.*

On the other hand, if there is no injustice, there is no justice. Wherever there is injustice, there is a need for judges. Some countries appoint judges via a judicial appointing committee or elections. In other countries, you can actually go to a judicial law school and get trained. This career path is usually only possible for people who already have a long careers in law behind them. If you want to become a judge, it's best to gain some experience in the legal corporate world. There are different types of court, such as the Court of Appeal and the High Court of Justice, so have a look at the relevant websites to receive a better understanding of what they are looking for. It is a hierarchical system that requires you to start at the bottom and work your way up as you gain the relevant experiences. This role mainly boils down to who you know and who acknowledges you – especially with elections and committees. There are often shadowing opportunities available, which can be a good start.

4.2.1.3 GOVERNMENTAL FUNCTIONS OR INSTITUTIONS

> *'Divide and rule, the politician cries; unite and lead, is watchword of the wise.'*
>
> *– Johann Wolfgang von Goethe*

A politician is someone who represents certain objectives for the country and conducts politics professionally, is active in government and usually an elected official. To become a politician, you must have a strong interest in how your country is governed and its processes. Therefore, join a political party if you want to start from entry level – preferably a prominent one. You will need to become popular in the local community and understand its particular requirements. To become listed, you usually need a certain number of signatures for your petition. What makes you want to be a politician? I believe it all starts innocently with fighting for humanity or justice, which will later shift to a desire to exercise power. Thus, when you have already done some high-powered jobs, it is easier to get involved within the government or institutions because of your 'powerful' background and experience. It is a career switch many people make after they have had some success. Although serving your country is not highly paid, it is very prestigious.

4.2.1.4 CONSULTANT

> *'To think well and to consent to obey someone giving good advice are the same thing'*
>
> *– Herodotus*

Being a consultant is very similar to being a lawyer. You need the problem-solving skills, the analytical mind and the ability to work as part of a team. However, you will not be working on the legal side of things. Generally, you will have several departments that have a core focus on strategy, delivery, business development, etc. in a specialised field. It could be that your team will be positioned to analyse the company as a chief executive. Consulting companies serve clients at every level of their organisations. Therefore, you will be working more with models, statistics and strategies. This can be applied to a wide range of sectors.

4.2.1.5 BANKER

> *'A banker is a fellow that lends you his umbrella when the sun is shining, but wants it back the minute it begins to rain.'*
>
> *– Mark Twain*

This quote made me laugh because there is a perception that bankers are greedy. The reality is that they are people who have learnt how money works. Within a bank, you have different departments such as retail and business banking, corporate banking, wealth and investment management, and private banking. You can start working at a bank as a paralegal and later be trained as an in-house lawyer or work in the compliance or risk department if you desire to touch upon the legal and risk side of a bank. The financial world mainly deals with white-collar crime and fraud, such as insider trading.

4.2.1.6 ACADEMIC

> *'Academic success depends on research and publications'*
> *– Philip Zimbardo*

This quote says it all in a nutshell. As an academic, you will be doing devoted research for a certain project at the faculty department and will hopefully get your work published. It requires a lot of discipline and long hours behind the desk. The advantage is you will have more holidays than all the above-mentioned professions. It's like being a student for life, only on a more serious note. You will spend your time researching, sending drafts, going to conferences and publishing your work. In the meantime, you can teach students about the topics you're writing about or advise the business world on certain matters. Getting a job within the academic world is all about who you know, your qualifications and your publications.

4.2.1.7 ENTREPRENEUR

> *'It's fine to celebrate success, but it is more important to heed the lessons of failure.'*
> *– Bill Gates*

As an entrepreneur, you need to have a good tolerance for failure and confidence in your capabilities. You need to believe religiously that your business is going to work and not overthink things. Entrepreneurs have an idea and go to work on it. You will need to know your own mind and be ready for whatever obstacles stand in your way. Law school will teach you to think systematically, see every angle of a situation and have the developed ability to anticipate multiple scenarios. You can never cover them all. You should look at successful entrepreneurs within your industry to learn from their mistakes and find out what works in the business. From a legal perspective, you need to get to know your business, have good client contacts and a strong team. Start with a business plan, know your industry, build a brand, open communication lines and get a good team together. There are so many books and websites that you can easily get lost in them. Once you have your idea and feel like putting it to work, your journey as an entrepreneur will begin.

4.3 Differences between law firms

Each law firm has its own specialisation or reputation within a certain area. The twenty-fourth Rule of Law School is: *understand the differences between law firms*. Conduct a search on which professions and law firms specialise in your favourite course. This will help you to understand better what lies ahead and what you would like to do. The conventional route in law is as follows: go to law school; get some experience in the legal sector; graduate; train at a prestigious law firm; stay there for a couple of years, and then maybe move to another firm for a higher position as senior associate or partner. This is what your career path might comprise.

There are differences between working for a US firm and a UK firm. US firms tend to have smaller teams, fewer support functions and therefore bigger earnings. Thus, on the one hand, you'll get more exposure; on the other hand, you'll be less able to outsource the 'dirty' work. UK firms have larger teams and provide more support so you can focus on the core of the business. However, you will make slightly less money.

There are several questions you can ask the recruiter:

- What are the differences between working (for example) for Freshfields and working for Linklaters? Obviously, they will describe the culture of their firm. Probe them further on the style of working and their approaches.
- How is the work delegated and what is the split of the work? In other words, how does the practice group of, for example, the corporate branch operate on every level?
- What will be expected of you in terms of performance? This is dependent on the partner of a certain practice group; direct your questions to distinguish these.
- How are billable hours determined and what happens when there is not enough work? Have they been expanding lately or downsizing?
- Does the company allow you to have a work-life balance?
- How does the firm invest in personal progression and development?
- What are good questions to ask after an interview? This is key!
- What type of remuneration or promotion system is there?

Every firm has a different promotion and remuneration system. There are two main types of structure within law firms: the lockstep model and the milestone path or merit base system. In a lockstep model, which is the traditional model, you will get promoted according to the number of years you have been working at the firm. With the relatively new milestone system, you will be assessed based on your competencies. The latter depends on how well you perform within the firm, meaning how well you get along with the team, partners and clients, as well as your individual technical contribution. Most firms are moving towards a milestone system, and this is a good question to ask your recruiter because you need to understand that the larger the firm is, the longer it will take you to get promoted. This is due to the amount of business, the availability of positions and the fierce competition.

Nowadays, you also have virtual law firms where there are no bricks and mortar, and you will be working from home. This allows you to have a more flexible working style and less commute. This concept mainly works for lawyers who are further down the line in their careers, such as senior associates and partners. You will have an online system, a meeting place for you and your clients and virtual support. There will be a telephone receptionist who actually deals with your enquiries. These types of firms have been created to retain people who want a better work-life balance.

4.4 What are law firms looking for?

Obtaining good to excellent grades is paramount. This is the first filter that law firms apply to the incoming applications. Obviously it is a mix of skill set they are looking for; however, the first thing a recruiter does when filtering the large pile of applications is based on grades. To increase the chances of being accepted into a top-notch law firm you need to have at least a commendation or any other standard the law firm specifically requires.[13] When this is not explicitly stated on the website, do pick up the phone and call the firm you are interested in. This is a good way of introducing yourself to the law firm and getting

---

13 This is dependent on the law firm and could change.

acquainted with them. Make sure you leave a lasting positive impression of your personality and character.

Law firms are also looking for candidates with some form of experience, so you can also show you are a hard worker. This gives you a good way of demonstrating that you understand the business you're about to enter and that you possess commercial awareness. Work experience also develops you as a person and teaches you to put theory into practice. The best experience to gain is in the legal sector or in the law society at your university.

As a lawyer, your drafting skills need to be excellent. Therefore, it is important to score high on your dissertation and maybe even to write something for a legal magazine. There are plenty of legal student unions who are looking for volunteer writers. This is where the attention to detail is important. They will test your drafting skills in your interview rounds. You need to be able to spot ambiguities and errors. Working at a top international law firm requires dealing with highly confidential deals. Decision-making on a daily basis must be compliant with what the law firm expects and promises to deliver to the client. This is why gaining experience is crucial! Your decision-making needs to be in line with what is expected of you in the commercial world. Yes, you are a student now with little experience; nevertheless, you want to distinguish yourself from the crowd and demonstrate your capabilities. Therefore, you must reach your highest potential if you would like to join a large international law firm.

If you want to join a mid- to small-sized firm, you do need similar qualities. However, the expectations are lower in terms of grades. You still need to show your ability in drafting and making a cultural fit though. The best way to discover this is to look at the graduate recruitment websites. Call them and ask questions. This will show eagerness, and it will also give you an opportunity to practise behaving like a professional. The twenty-fifth Rule of Law School is: *making a good impression can give you an advantage in the interview; be yourself, be kind, be polite and be professional.*

When you make the first phone call, you might be super nervous. I recommend writing down a script so you know in advance what to say. Practise it in the mirror and make sure you come across as confident. Call the least desired law firm you are considering first or just one you do not really want to work for. This will help you get over your fear, and you will see that the second, third and fourth phone call will be way more natural and professional. This method prepares you for an interview. Once you know the law firm, you will feel more at ease speaking with the people who work there, and they will like you more because you're relaxed. The last thing recruiters want is someone who is nervous and sweaty. That's a real no-no!! Don't be afraid to talk to them or to make mistakes. In the legal professional world, you need to be bold, sharp, friendly and professional. In short, the twenty-sixth Rule of Law School is: *come across like you are the candidate they have been looking for!*

CHAPTER 5

Get the job

The main reason for going to law school is to increase your chances of getting the job you want. Let me emphasise again: your degree is NOT a guarantee you will get the job you want!! You have to start early and make a plan. Don't worry if you don't know exactly what you want. Life is a journey, and we live long enough to make several careers. Just start with what you think is best for you, your future and developing your skill set.

Nowadays, most people in the western world have access to universities, meaning that we also have an inflation of intellectual knowledge. That is why I keep on hammering the point that you need to gain some form of experience, and I have described above which ones are the most useful and time efficient. I would also advise you to avoid getting into too much debt. This is a mistake many have made during their university years.

You should not take debt lightly when you are studying. Once you have finished your studies, you will still have many expenses that will put pressure on your bank balance. Therefore, try to raise some money with your family, start a business or work alongside your studies. Not only do you need to be a provider for yourself; you might one day be a provider for others. It's all about mindset obviously; however, I would advise you not to borrow more than 50% of your fees. It makes it easier for you to pay off your debt. You will decrease your pay-off tremendously, and that will give you breathing space to build for yourself and your family. The twenty-seventh Rule of Law School is: *make a financial plan to identify where you can decrease your costs and increase your income in order to have little or no debt when you graduate.*

After you finish university, you might want to go travelling, buy a house, drive a car, enjoy parties and more. These things become more expensive because your standards will most likely increase once you are a young professional. Above all, your parents will not be getting any younger, and you might need to support them and others one day. You might even be thinking about starting your own family. Okay calm down – this summary is just giving you a heads up and obviously you need to focus on one thing at a time. So, let's focus on how you can increase your likelihood of getting a job.

5.1 Networking

This is the first step towards getting the job you want. Be surrounded by the people you would like to work with, and the opportunities will come to you. This has to be conducted in a professional way because sometimes you get only one shot in a lifetime. So here are some tips and tricks you can use:

- **Plan your events.** I set a target of attending at least one networking event per month and gaining at least two new useful contacts. These events allow your conversations to extend further than a few simple interview questions. You can focus on events and people that fascinate you, so your conversations will have a more natural flow.

- **Do NOT interrupt conversations.** When a group of people are talking in a circle, just be present, smile and look at the person who is talking. You can join in the conversation later when the opportunity arises. It is natural for people to get irritated when they get interrupted, so be soft when approaching people. It is actually a good thing to be shy in the beginning because it makes other people feel stronger and they will be happy to start a conversation with you.

- **Walk around the room.** When a conversation is not heading in the direction you want, just excuse yourself to go and get a drink – do ask everyone you were talking to if they would like to have a drink too[14] – or go to the bathroom, etc. Walk through the room looking for someone who might be potentially interesting to talk to and approach that person with diplomacy. Do not cling on to your buddy you went with because you already know each other!

- **Be dynamic.** Understand that having a conversation with someone is an experience. The way you behave will be your business card for how people perceive you. Don't talk too much about yourself and don't let the other person dominate the conversation – even if they have a high rank. Allow and create dynamics in a conversation. This will be appreciated if done properly. If you run out of things to say, here are some ideas that could keep things going:

    - Ask your conversation partner how they came across the event and whether they know many people there. If they do, tell them what you're looking for and perhaps they can introduce you to the right person. This depends on how good your rapport with that person is.
    - Show an interest in the other party in terms of what they do and what their key responsibilities are. Ask

14 This will make people think well of you – obviously when there is an open bar.

what made them decide to go into law (or whatever their occupation is). Ask them about the challenges they deal with and the hours they work.

– Paying compliments to the event and actually forming an opinion can start a good debate, which will trigger an interesting conversation and draw more people to you. Ask if there is a mailing list or what the next event will be or if there are other events that are worth attending. If it isn't as good as other events you have attended, make a complimentary remark so you will show genuine interest in being there – just try to be positive.

– Learn to talk about your dreams or vision. Tell people what you would like to do and who you would like to become. People who share these dreams will be attracted to you, and you will end up being surrounded by like-minded people. Feel positive when you talk about it!!

• **Don't get tipsy or drunk! That's a no-no!** I have been to so many network drinks where people drank too much. This does not leave a positive impression. You might regret it if you lose control of your tongue and end up laying drunk on the carpet! Although it might be funny, you will not improve your career prospects at all. You will increase the likelihood of the 'why the hell did I just say or do that' moment. The only exception is when it's a cultural way of doing business; such as with Russians, when I would say: 'Nostrovia!'

• **Bring your business card.** Yes, even as a student you need a business card. Some websites do it for free, and even if you have to pay, it's a good investment. Firstly, you will come across as a professional. Secondly, it will show you actually want to stay in touch. Lastly, it's easier for you. Obviously, make sure your LinkedIn and Google search results are presentable. Remember, you live in a digital world, and your social footprint is there for all to see.

- **Pay attention.** If someone is talking to you, please do not look around for a better person to talk to. It's rude! Just excuse yourself or give your undivided attention to the person talking. Look people in the eyes when you get introduced and receive them with a smile. This sounds super basic; however, I do see people doing it wrong!

Networking is fun and never the same. In every form of business, it's important WHO you know and HOW you come across.

5.2 CV and cover letter

Your CV and cover letter will be your sales pitch to get the job you want. Therefore, it needs to be the best representation of your accomplishments and experience that is compliant with the position you are applying for. The length should only be one to two pages. Make sure your timeline is in reverse chronological order. It must be simple, clear and well structured. The content must be error-free, accurate and easy to read. It is okay to use different headings; however, do stick to one font. You can build up a structure by adding bullet points, columns and spacing. The twenty-eighth Rule of Law School is: *when you are writing your CV and cover letter, bear in mind to whom you are writing and **how you can add value for them**.*

Start by reading the job description intensively, and note down the most important skills required and buzzwords. Your goal is to make your CV and cover letter compatible with the job description. For EVERY legal application, ALWAYS emphasise that you have an eye for detail because this is an essential skill in law. Don't replicate what is on your CV in your cover letter. What you need to do in your cover letter is emphasise your most relevant experiences in relation to the job specification. You should explain how this experience shaped you, what type of skills you enhanced or gained, what the outcome was and how this improved you. The tone of your letter is very important. Try to avoid standard letter openings because you will bore the recruiter and fail to stand out.

If you don't get the job, you need to work continuously on improving your CV and cover letter. Once you have submitted an application, follow it up. Some of the firms will tell you they don't provide feedback due to large numbers. Do not insist on getting feedback because you will be regarded as a time waster.

Here is an example of what I think a CV should look like:[15]

---

15 Pleae note that on A4 paper this CV should consist of two pages.

Daniela Vinkeles Melchers
+ 44 78 7777 7778, vinkelesmelchers@mail.com

My experience has given me transferable skills, especially in negotiations, problem solving, leadership and management. I possess highly developed communication skills; for example, I speak five languages and believe that active listening is crucial to understanding the customer in order to provide the best service. Additionally, I learn very quickly from others and adapt easily to circumstances.

EDUCATION AND QUALIFICATIONS

City University Law School, London
Master in International Commercial Law (2:1)   201.

University of Amsterdam Business School, Amsterdam
Audit Business Studies (2:1)   201.

University of Amsterdam Law Faculty, Amsterdam
Bachelor in Law (2:1)   200.

WORK EXPERIENCE

Freshfields Bruckhaus Deringer,   Oct 2014 – p
Legal Recruitment, London
Working as a legal sourcing specialist in an international magic cir
firm where the focus is on track fee-earning and non-fee-earning
with the aim to bring them on board.

Legal Sourcing Specialist
Achievement: Highest volume of sourcing on LI on a structural bas
demonstrated proactive and positive mental attitude by introdu
notice board, three bullet point structure for meetings and sending interim
reports to manager.

- Overseeing global sourcing strategy within the legal market and s
  desired talent to create leads. Using different sourcing channels
- Making and building contacts via phone or LinkedIn and managing/
  qualifying all the external potential candidates.
- Ensuring updates in the internal system concerning status, notes and
  developments using various systems and methods.
- Coordinating the day-to-day running of headhunting with strict
  time-management.
- Keeping up to date with the developments in the legal market.

EXTRA CURRICULAR ACTIVITIES

Allen and Overy & Leonardo Co., Law Firm, Amsterdam   **2013**
Competitive two-day course where law students had to collaborate with
finance students in order to establish and pitch the best merger deal for
the partners of the firm.

Business Course Lawyer

Achievement: Chosen to present and pitch the outcome of our analyses to partners and associates.

Use active words so your personality does come across.

- Competed to enter the business course on Mergers and Acquisitions.
- Researched and negotiated on strategic legal and financial level with the clients and competitors to generate information in an accurate and timely manner.
- Prepared, wrote and negotiated the pitch proposal.

UNISCA Foundation, International Politics, Amsterdam   **Oct 2012–Oct 2013**

A simulation of the United Nations organised by the University of Amsterdam for university students worldwide. Participated as ICJ Lawyer, and later asked to join the board as the member responsible for marketing, PR, locations and socials.

PR and Event Manager

Achievement: Developed a passion for planning, designing and dealing with international governmental issues.

Show results and measurements where you can.

- *PR*: Increased participants by 25% using more effective time-management.
- Promoted the programme nationally and internationally.
- Coordinated the contents of the marketing materials such as website, brochures, posters, flyers and adverts.
- Created a new image by working on selling points and outlook.
- Attended meetings, network events and competitor events.

Event: Venue search, maintaining contact and dealing with the contracts.

- Managed a team of seven people.

Alibi, Legal Magazine, University of Amsterdam, Amsterdam   **Aug 2011–Sep 2012**

Chairwoman

Achievement: Created a flow in submissions from writers and readers. Orchestrated interviews with high-profile people within the legal sector.

- Recruited and led a team of six people.
- Introduced a new brand and strategy designed to attract sponsorship.
- Introduced and organised legal training. Tasks included designing training programmes, booking venues, inviting lecturers and attracting target groups.
- Coordinated the graphic designs, sponsorship and marketing.
- Established a new website to monitor needs.
- Created new positions in and around the organisation.
- Built strong relationships with external suppliers, writers and readers.

Treasurer
Achievement: Developed leadership skills by taking responsibility, looking at the bigger picture of the company and becoming confident with numbers.

- Designed financial statements, tax and account management.
- Got the magazine out of debt and built up credit.

AWARD AND SKILLS

Depending on the awards, you can also mention them after your education – this is a matter of choice.

Award: Best Debater at Lagerhuis Debate, UN & me. **2012**

Languages: Native Dutch; fluent English and German; conversational Spanish; and French.

This is a huge asset at a firm and that's why I would recommend you to at least try to learn another language.

Certificates:
German Advanced, City University **2014**
Academic English, IELTS 7.0 & Delegation of Germany LIMUN **2013**
ICJ Lawyer, UNISCA **2012**
Legal Typing Master Test Certificate **2010**

Start with your contact details so recruiters can easily reach you. Then briefly introduce yourself, showing how you distinguish yourself from the competition and why you are THE must-call-back candidate. This should be done in three lines, and it needs to be catchy, professional and impressive! If you don't know what to write, ask the three closest people in your life what you are good at. This will give you some inspiration for your writing. Nobody gets it right the first time. Just get some skills on paper and keep on developing it into a brief summary until you're satisfied. This is an opportunity for you to emphasise the key competencies required for the role. Make sure you're the right person for the role or at least make sure you are an applicant who is worth their time.

In the second paragraph, you should state your education, and this must contain your average grade. You can submit full details of your subject grades in an attachment. Law firms are looking for people who have an eye for detail, and that will be reflected in the level of your grades. If you are applying, for example, for a role as a family law paralegal, then include the grade you obtained for family law. These are small and simple adjustments to make and will help the recruiter to get straight to the point.

You should list your work experience first if it is more relevant than your extra-curricular experience. Obviously, you need to prioritise your CV according to the relevancy. In your summary, make sure you start with the last experience you gained. When you have gaps, just state briefly what you have been doing – this is mainly applicable for candidates who have already graduated and still not managed to receive a training contract. When you cannot find a role in the legal world, I would highly recommend trying to work for a client of the law firm you are interested in. For example, Freshfields' biggest client in London is the Bank of England, and Linklaters works closely with Glencore within the UK. These are alternative routes to trigger the entrepreneurial lawyer inside of you.

In the last paragraph, you should include awards, skills and interests. In the legal world, achievement and personality are crucial because it is a service industry. That's why you must understand the culture of the firm. Some firms have staff skiing trips while others support certain charities or artists. Others value awards – this can be anything from becoming captain at your golf club, to gaining a certificate at a conference or winning a prestigious debate.

Some universities do offer services to help improve your CV. I think their usefulness depends on the recruiters. Most of them don't really go in depth because they have no incentive to do so. What I would suggest is to go to a reputable recruitment agency. They will have a subscription process where you will physically meet them. If a recruiter does not require this, I would not necessarily recommend going through that agency.

Ask them what they think of your CV and how you could improve it. If they give a vague answer, ask them what would make your CV outstanding. Ask them what type of experience you need to gain. Be careful with agencies when asking the latter question because they have an interest in pushing you into certain roles, and they will not necessarily act in your interest. They make money when they place you successfully for a role, so they will be more than willing to help you to get that particular role. You should also ask for the recruiters' background and experience because that can give you a good indication of what your chances will be on the market. Who are their clients? What are the current market conditions? What do I have to do to get a job?

An honest recruiter will tell you to apply directly to a firm because the recruitment process for a law firm is cheaper. They would not need to pay a recruiter; therefore, an equally good candidate found via the direct recruitment process prevails. Finding work is a full-time job, and you need to break down the market so that your efforts are targeted in the right areas. What I do is make a spreadsheet with all the interesting law firms and their vacancies, and mark them with colours to record their status. For example:

Law Firm	Application	Role	Contact	Deadline
Freshfields	Applied	Litigation Paralegal	Partner D. Brown	21-09-2019
Linklaters	In process	Banking Litigation Paralegal	Associate M. Steiner	25-09-2019

You can add more columns and your training contract application. I preferred to keep mine separate because they are two different applications. Having a list to cross off will make you feel more motivated and in control of your applications. Search through LinkedIn to see who is connected to useful people so you can find out who your contact will be. You should know by now that law is pretty much based on WHO you know. So, if there are contacts in your circle, by all means use them; however, just make sure you are the type of person they want to be referring. As I mentioned before, reputation is paramount. If you approach people by email, check your messages thoroughly for mistakes.

When you send out your application, I recommend converting your CV into a PDF file. The reason is that the recipient might use a different program that can cause your CV to look like a complete mess. With a PDF file, you will avoid conversion problems. Your CV is your sales pitch, so you had better suit up.

There are many different types of cover letters for different types of applications. You should always conduct your research on cover letter examples from reliable sources such as reputable university websites. Read at least three of them in order to create winning content that contains a diversity of verbs and terminology. You don't need to use over-complicated words that were only used during the Roman Empire – recruiters don't want to be confused. Just make sure the paragraphs are structured according to their relevance. The twenty-ninth Rule of Law School is: *write a clear, well-structured and typo-free CV and cover letter, and keep on improving your content when you do not get the results you are expecting.* Above all, be motivated!

See Appendix 8.2 for an example of how I think an impactful and clear cover letter should look. Preferably address the person rather than writing "Dear Sir/Madam" or "To whom it may concern".

Your cover letter needs to be persuasive, well-structured, clear and flawless. It is your opportunity to communicate your individuality, enthusiasm, professional strengths and background. You should tailor the letter to match the requirements of the job you are applying for. For example, if you are applying for a non-governmental position, show how you have been involved and what skills you gained. It is good to talk about your dreams, passions and dedication – this is what most employers want to hear, and it will give them a positive impression.

Writing a cover letter is a test of your writing and persuasion skills – in particular when you are applying for a job where influencing skills are required. You must aim to create a true impact – go for the wow effect! Not a lot of people can actually do this, so having this mindset will put you ahead of the competition.

The format should be conservative and set out as a business letter. Even when you submit your application in a box,[16] do stick to the requirements. This demonstrates your eye for detail. When you are applying for a role abroad, make sure you do research on how letters are written in that particular country. Every country has different rules and styles on how to address an employer.

"I would prefer to just look at your resume."

16 Meaning when you cannot upload your letter and need to type out your cover letter in the given space.

5.3 Interview

An invitation for an interview means you have got your foot in the door. If you managed to get invited, well done!! So how do you prepare for the interview? The best way is to place yourself in the shoes of the interviewer and make sure you have a confident, positive mindset.

Firstly, you will need to know what they are looking for and what they want to hear. Obviously, you need to do your research. As a law student, it is expected that you will know the company inside out – the more you know, the more confident the recruiter will be to hire you. The culture of some firms will require you to be humble and kind, while others will be looking for someone who is bold and daring.

The particular competencies required for the role are crucial, and you need to be able to demonstrate that your skills, experience and personality fit the firm. Be prepared to demonstrate your skill set and elaborate with specific examples. Make sure you understand the question to avoid waffling and take your time to think about how to structure your answer. This is also a test of how you cope with pressure and how coherently you can answer on the spot. In every example or challenge you wish to elaborate on, make sure you have a positive lesson learned from it. This allows the recruiter to have a better understanding of your way of thinking.

Here are some subject areas in which questions could be asked in your interview:

5.3.1 Technical ability: meeting deadlines and delivering results

This is the analytical part where you have to demonstrate that you can do the job. You will be tested on how you develop your ideas. The types of questions you can expect are:

Tell me about your study that you undertook on your own initiative. Were there any challenges involved?

Could you demonstrate that you are eager to develop professional skills? How do you keep up to date with developments?

5.3.2 Teamwork and effective communication

In law – and indeed in business in general – one of the foundations of success is building effective working relationships. In a demanding environment, you will be spending lots of time with your colleagues, and you will need to be a good communicator. The types of questions you can expect are:

Could you give me a specific example when you demonstrated adaptability in a situation where someone had a different personal style? How did you deal with it?

Can you think of an occasion when you had a conflicting or challenging situation? What did you learn from it?

5.3.3 Commercial awareness

The core of your work will be to understand the clients and work towards the business objectives. You need to be able to cope with the commercial environment, and it's crucial to see the bigger picture and maintain a balance between the firm/ team and the client.

How do you keep up to date with the legal sector? Can you tell me about one of our deals?

What do you think of the deal? How does it meet the objectives of the corporation and distinguish it from competitors?

Think about some of our clients. How would you maintain a quality service? How do you deal with impatient clients?

5.3.4 Organisation and management

With the skill set of organisation and management, you can elaborate on personal growth – how you manage and respond within highly pressured environments. Your answers will reflect how you adapt to situations and show leadership.

Could you describe a high-pressured environment you had to deal with? How did you respond and cope with the situation?

Tell me about a situation when you demonstrated resilience and tenacity?

The above examples give you an idea of what the recruiters have in mind for interviews. This is just a guide, and you should prepare yourself for a wider range of questions. At the end, they will allow you to ask questions, and this is one of the most crucial parts in the interview because it shows the direction of your mind and whether you have done your research. The better the questions, the more you will impress the recruiter. Ask questions on the team structure, travel possibilities, charity (if connected), etc. DO NOT ask questions on salary, bonus, pension or benefit packages in the first round. Save that until the last round.

CHAPTER 6

Law school ratio decidendi

Robert Bourns, 172nd president of the Law Society of England and Wales and former senior partner

Robert Bourns is a very traditional yet pragmatic man. After embarking on the conventional route of law, he was appointed as president of the Law Society. How do you become the president of the Law Society? Mr Bourns points out how paramount work experience is for a successful legal career. Without work experience, you will not truly understand what career will suit you best or what skill set you need to be focused on.

Mr Bourns learned what path to embark upon during his rotational training for becoming a lawyer. "In practice you will see what areas emphasise certain skill sets," he said. One of the skills he has developed the most is advocacy. This skill, if mastered correctly, allows you to communicate clearly and concisely. Furthermore, Mr Bourns recommends all students to go to a well-established university and become involved with pro-bono work in order to access the judicial system. One of his philosophies that guided him through law school and his career is to make sure you are in a 'win-win situation'.

The legal industry is highly competitive; therefore, it is important to be resilient, think ahead, keep your options open, speak to professionals and pursue the right experiences. Even if you are not sure of which path to embark on, begin by saying yes to opportunities and getting involved in legal affairs. Being too measured does not always pay off. Mr Bourns advises that when you grab an opportunity with two hands, "know that if you're a success, you're kept, and if you don't progress as much, you're out". His sober analysis is the consequence of years learning about the sector and its pressures.

Susan Hingley, paralegal at international law firms

Susan decided to go to law school because she knew she would make good money after she graduated. She was attracted to the prestige and the amount of money you can acquire after getting a law degree. Deep in her heart, she always wanted to be an actress; however, it was difficult to make much money doing that. Therefore, she chose to go to law school first and then obtain her diploma at drama school.

After completing her Bachelor in Law at Warwick University (UK), she obtained her Legal Practice Course (LPC) at the University of Law in Bloomsbury. In the UK, the LPC is one of the most common routes to receive a training contract at a law firm.[17] During her bachelor's she was not always motivated, and only got inspired by ambitious people she studied with. Her advice to you is this: "Surround yourself with the ambitious people at law school and study with them."

17 LPC is equivalent to a Master in Law programme in other countries.

She regrets not participating in any of the Model United Nations (MUN) programmes because "this is a fun way of meeting ambitious people or gaining experience in public speaking or other skills that could be of use". Her second tip is this: "Sign up for any Erasmus programmes to go abroad or participate in extra-curricular activities such as MUNs."

During the LPC, you learn a more practical side of law and how to apply it. Susan's advice is to "really prepare and plan your studies properly – it will avoid overload of work and give you a sense of control". Susan signed up to work at the Citizens Advice Bureau. This work experience allowed her to deal with real-life problems of individuals in society. "It makes your studies truly more vivid," she said.

Susan is now working as an actress alongside projects run by prestigious international law firms. She concluded our interview with this insight: "Not only does a degree from law school increase your value in the marketplace, it actually helped me in my acting career as a person. You do gain analytical thinking and organisation skills that are invaluable for a lifetime!"

Professor Carl Stychin, dean of the City Law School, University of London

Professor Stychin is a man who knows university life inside out. He gave me very good advice on how to write a good legal piece and outlined the mental attitude of a good student. He has eight publications to his name, runs a law school and has experience at over six different universities globally.

He believes that the foundation of legal writing is doing research properly. He still believes in the old way of doing research:

starting in the library. Here, he says, you can find the books on the topics if given or just get inspired when you need to come up with a topic. He advises that you find a topic that is **new** for your dissertation and take the following steps:

Understand the issue in question to narrow down the content you are looking for. Then find all the case law regarding the topic and make sure you are updated with the referrals. Keep reading, and spend time on your own to really absorb the field correctly. Follow this by mapping out the road you want to head down. When you are done, get all your knowledge on paper – **anything.**

Before you start writing, make sure you eliminate the mental barriers you might be challenged by. Find your ideal place, time, food – even if that means not getting dressed, that's fine – just be you. Don't criticise yourself; just fill in the paper: go, go, go!

Once you've finished and have nothing to write about anymore, try to make a beginning, a middle and an end. If you have the opportunity, lie down and test your own arguments. When you're ready, you'll start crafting. This takes the most time. The information you presented on paper needs to be crafted into sentences that make sense and are not too long. Your ideas need to be clearly stated and elaborated with examples, consequences or any other factors that would make the subject in question more interesting; keep it tidy though. You should divide the text into different sections to give the reader a better overview of the relevant subsections.

The most important tip Professor Stychin gives you is this: "Make sure you understand the basic writing rules." That means knowing the proper construction of a sentence and the basic rules of grammar and style. Every word in your dissertation, thesis or any other legal writing needs to possess significance. The biggest mistake students make is trying to fill up the paper with words and no actual content. In short, tighten your ideas with words that actually provide substantive content. Often, when you re-read your work, many sentences can be left out, and the same point can still be made.

What do you do when you are having a bad day and no inspiration? Don't be too hard on yourself, and allow yourself, as Professor Stychin calls it, "a mental health day". This is a day where you take care of yourself and do things that make you happy. This should be temporary. Another valuable tip he gives is to learn how to give your best when things in your life are going wrong. This is key to making yourself successful in almost every career.

After having an insightful conversation about writing, I had to ask Professor Stychin what he actually does as a dean of a law school? He laughed and told me that many people ask him that question – even his own mother. He explained that being a dean of a law faculty is very different from being a professor. The environment is more fast-paced, and you are attending many meetings or events. You need to talk to the staff to understand what's going on, what can be improved and how to maintain the performance. The performance is measured by the quality of the courses, safety of the university, exam processes, complaints, staff grievances and the range of programmes being offered to prospective candidates. You're shaping the vision of the law faculty, and you have to think very strategically. Therefore, your job is to be **always** responsible for the law faculty.

In conclusion, Professor Stychin wants prospective law students to know that some wisdom comes with time, and the older you get, the more time you take to reflect so as to avoid making the same mistake twice. He believes that everyone should be their true self and translate it into action.

Rachael Williams, financial ombudsman

Rachael Williams finished the bar, practised for a few years as a barrister, became a solicitor, pursued a master's degree and now works at the Financial Ombudsman Service.

How did you achieve success during law school? Law school was quite intimidating, and Ms Williams decided she needed to build confidence to overcome her trepidation. She did this by understanding what she was good at and by maintaining a confident attitude, even in those areas where she did not excel. She chose to go to law school because she liked advocacy and wanted to create a more detailed mind.

What study method do you recommend? Ms Williams recommends all law students truly learn how to plan and organise their work. You know how much time you have in a year, when your exams are and what your strengths and weaknesses are. Ms Williams' tip to current law students is to keep a structured routine. Deal with your studies as if it were a job. When you treat it like a job, where you stick to your prescribed lunch hour, you will earn yourself fun, extracurricular time and actually enjoy it. Make good notes, read the booklets and take a revision course. If you need to be isolated, make sure you are. If you need a break, take a walk. You cultivate an analytical mind by asking yourself questions, and, if you cannot answer, you will have someone who helps you at the revision course. When you are writing an essay, keep a structure in mind. First: what is the point? Give an example – assess the situation and answer the question by keeping the point in mind. Make sure all that you write is relevant.

What were the challenges with becoming a lawyer? The interviews are often designed to intimidate you to see how you think on your feet. As a lawyer, you need to deal with unexpected situations. Her advice is to stay calm, capture the bigger picture and be yourself. This is hard to practise on your own; however, it helps to prepare yourself for an 'intellectual challenge'.

How do you know in advance which law firm suits you, in terms of culture? Ms Williams advises analysing the type of clients the firm takes. This will tell you a lot about what industries the firm is involved with and the type of work it deals in. You can find a lot of information in the Law Society magazines or just simply type in the firm's name on the (Supreme) Court website. Analyse the partners and the experiences they gained, and go to network events to hear what people say about the firms. That's why she recommends you to have a mentor – this can be anyone. There are many institutions that offer mentorship for when you have trouble finding one.[18]

Camilio Morales Saavedra, paralegal

Camilio studied for his LLB at the Pontifical Catholic University of Chile. He always enjoyed writing philosophical texts and has a big interest in how the government functions and what political impact certain regulations have on society. He chose to study law because he is a true humanist and wants to improve society. As he has an entrepreneurial side, he also believed that law would be more useful than subjects like sociology and international relations in terms of starting a business.

Once he began his studies, Camilio discovered that his expectations of how law school works were very different from the reality. "You need to be very serious compared to high school

---

18 Ask your university, the Law Society or other institutions that may offer these services.

and get yourself organised in planning your life," he said. He found the content to be very different and of a much higher volume than he had experienced previously.

His study method was to focus on one subject or course each week. For example, Week 6 would be dedicated to studying only contract law and Week 7 to criminal law. This helped him to gain a long-term memory. He believes it's essential that you see the bigger picture of the content, and you can train yourself to do this by first of all understanding the history and background of the case or regulations. The best thing he did was travelling after his studies because it taught him to look at the interior of society within its regulations and laws. He has now signed up to do his master in law which will be partially in Chile and partially in Germany.

Hannah Bennai, law student

Hannah shadowed a lawyer at Clifford Chance for a day during high school and was very much impressed by the professional standards. She thought it would be a good idea to become a legal secretary and discussed her ideas with her teacher. Due to her good grades, he advised her to become a lawyer.

She is currently an undergraduate studying law at Birkbeck University in London. She chose Birkbeck because it specialises in evening courses, and this allows her to work during the day as a paralegal. The hardest thing so far has been finding a balance between work and study.

The best method of study for her is revising what she has learned at the end of each week. She recommends making the best notes you can during classes and gaining confidence in asking questions. "You study law because you want to be there, so make your time useful and don't worry what other people think of you before asking a question," she said. We agreed that the students who act most confidently in class don't necessarily know more than everyone else. She prefers writing notes to improve her memory.

When she needs to write essays or coursework, she first reads the question and then researches the topic. In order to get her thoughts on paper, the first draft of her essay is completed confidently and without too much self-criticism. She then leaves her writing for a few days while she does more research, and eventually returns to it with a more critical eye – as if she were the teacher who will be marking it.

Hannah has already started applying for training contracts and will do her master's once she has obtained her LLB degree. She received an award from the Law Society of England for the best tort law result.

Laura Cucchiara, lawyer

Laura studied Law and Business at Bocconi University in Milan, Italy. The exams there are conducted both in writing and orally.

She used to be very shy and had difficulty memorising the content of her law books. When she started studying in a group, her grades improved a lot. To improve your skills at law school, she recommends you do all your reading. At the end of each week or month, you should recap with your classmates what you've learned in order to gain a true understanding. She recommends that a group should be no larger than four people.

Later on, she decided to go abroad to study in Vienna. This experience helped her personality and character to develop and blossom. Moreover, this new university offered her a different range of courses than her first university. Bocconi had links with the Erasmus programme, so the transfer was quite easy.

Following her time at the University of Vienna, she applied to the United Nations through her university and got herself an internship in Vienna which she enjoyed very much. She learned that international organisations are very grade focused and only want to recruit the cream of the crop. She next applied to the European Commission – again through her university. During this experience, she learned that dedication, hard work and kind people are the most important ingredients for productivity. Therefore, she says, you should always try to surround yourself with positive people. She even met her current husband during her internship at the European Commission and is now happily married.

Her most important piece of advice is to do your research on what a university has to offer you. When you apply, check in advance what you need to do in order to have a successful application. An additional experience not only develops your character; it also teaches you how to deal with different types of examination.

When you are not sure what area of the law profession you are working towards, she recommends that you write your dissertation from a legal comparative viewpoint. For example, you can approach a topic from a civil as well as a criminal law perspective. In her opinion, criminal law is really for tough people, and you need to develop a thick skin to deal with those types of cases on a daily basis. She wasn't sure that would be for her, so she decided to keep civil law as an option.

CHAPTER 7

Rules of law school

1. Have a positive reason for being at law school.

2. You must be willing to work hard, develop skills and be the type of student the university is looking for.

3. Know how to deal with a pile of books.

4. See the bigger picture.

5. Honour thy intellectual colour drawing.

6. Know how to conclude correctly in any circumstance of the case.

7. Make legal writing your second nature.

8. Know the relevant FACTS!

9. No matter how thin the coin is, it always has two sides.

10. Start with the end in mind.

11. The bibliography must reflect your understanding of how to do academic research.

12. Cite **all** sources in footnotes.

13. Score high, even when the expectations are low.

14. Go abroad!

15. Do your due diligence carefully.

16. Make sure you distinguish yourself from other applicants.

17. Write to at least five organisations that might help to fund your education.

18. Get both civil and common law study experiences.

19. You need experience with a reputable law firm on your CV.

20. Sign up with organisations to gain new experiences.

21. Your diploma is **NOT** a guarantee you will get the job you want.

22. Get good grades!

23. There are many more professions you can enter with a law degree besides law.

24. Understand the differences between law firms.

25. Making a good impression can give you an advantage in the interview; be yourself, be kind, be polite and be professional.

26. Come across like you are the candidate they have been looking for!

27. Make a financial plan to identify where you can decrease your costs and increase your income in order to have little or no debt when you graduate.

28. When you are writing your CV and cover letter, bear in mind to whom you are writing and **how you can add value for them**.

29. Write a clear, well-structured and typo-free CV and cover letter, and keep on improving your content when you do not get the results you are expecting.

CHAPTER 8

Appendices

8.1 Sample of a university application letter

Dear Sir/Madam,

It is my pleasure to apply for the Maritime Law master's programme at the University of . . . This area of law has always been my core focus, and I believe participating in your programme will allow me to bridge the gap between my academic and professional life and put maritime law into practice.

My passion for law started during my time at elementary school. I gave a presentation about the legal system in the Netherlands and how the court works. Ever since, it has been my desire to study law. During my bachelor's, I developed theoretical experience, and various disciplines reinforced my interest. Does the law protect victims or does it cover damages? How does the law serve justice? These and many other questions have fascinated me as the answers can be profoundly diverse. By analysing from judicial, social and economic perspectives, the conclusion will enrich a case. Even more intriguing is defending a position by cleverly arguing the points with a sense of morality. My attitude towards learning can be encapsulated in this Plato quotation: *"The direction in which education starts a man will determine his future life."*

I am particularly interested in the field of maritime law. While the *Deepwater Horizon* in the Gulf of Mexico was in the news and reporters alerted the world, nobody had the power to repress the spill. I felt the urge to expedite the catastrophic situation. This was my strongest turning point when I knew that I wanted to examine this kind of issue as often as possible. Subsequently, I chose my thesis subject to be civil liability for marine oil pollution damage. In advance, I want to analyse maritime law to ensure the path that I want to embark upon is the right one. Further into my writing I found more enthusiasm in analysing my thesis. Moreover, maritime law differs from other laws by the diversity of parties, damages and the consequences. This diversity corresponds to my personal traits: creative critical thinking, self-management, leadership and teamwork.

I have always adhered to the idea that true understanding of theory in highly analytical studies grows by implementing the acquired theory in practice. Currently, I am chairwoman and treasurer of the legal magazine *Alibi* at my faculty, and this has been invaluable to my development. The duties I fulfilled at *Alibi* were a challenge that I relished, and they acted as a springboard to take me to the next level. I learnt to create a productive team by sharing my ambition, communication/marketing skills and beneficial relationships with others. I started to publish articles in *Alibi* which enabled me to criticise and analyse judicial articles. I learned to record my thoughts in a clear and concise manner. This, in turn, helped me to write an excellent bachelor's thesis. For every edition I was seeking opportunities to reach the next level with the same budget and still be distinctive. From previous experience in radio and TV, creative thinking was blossoming, and working as a team helped me to share thoughts in a comprehensible and cogent manner on various different levels. Additionally, the results of my work were often made available for the general public, which placed an even greater emphasis on the importance of a comprehensive understanding of theory.

I have chosen to apply to your programme for many reasons. The two main reasons are: I will receive the best education in maritime law and I will be able to study together with brilliant minds who, like me, are driven by their ambition to become specialists in this area. Furthermore, the courses that are in the programme's curriculum are exactly the courses that I would like to specialise in. While writing my thesis, I identified that your university possesses outstanding professors. Role models are important for progressing to the next step in a career. In the future, I would like to work as a lawyer, and later in my career become an arbitration judge. My goal is to have the ability to learn new things in life; intellectually, emotionally and professionally. The best way to accomplish this is to enter the programme the University of . . . offers.

Alongside my studies, I participate in many sporting activities, play the violin, travel and I am fond of reading. I used to do contact sports, team sports and individual sports; from judo to hockey to horse riding. Since my childhood, I have taken part in summer camps where I could both develop new skills and contribute to society by, for example, collecting donations for charities. Also, I travelled all around the world with my family, visiting countries in Europe, Asia, America and elsewhere. During my travels I have always tried to master languages, and I now have command of Dutch, English, German, Spanish, French and Hebrew. My favourite books are the biography of Nelson Mandela and *Justice* by Michael Sandel.

I will demonstrate my devotion to education en route to obtaining a degree in Maritime Law at your university. The challenge of studying at your university is the one I desire the most.

Therefore, I sincerely hope to be invited for a personal interview so I can further elucidate my motivational letter and CV. I sincerely believe I fit the profile of a student of the Maritime Law programme and am very much looking forward to becoming a prospective student of the University of . . .

I am wholeheartedly looking forward to your reply and the upcoming academic year.

Yours faithfully,

Daniela Vinkeles Melchers

8.2 Example cover letters

8.2.1 *To a law firm via email*

Dear Sir/Madam,

I would like to express my interest as a potential candidate and offer you my service. Currently, I am in the latter stages of my LLM at City University. One of the LLM courses I took is International Arbitration,[19] and I am very keen to gain experience at the Dispute Resolution group. During my studies I got very familiar with electronic search engines. Last summer, I graduated from my LLB degree, and I have also actively audited a year of business studies. I have gained analytic and numerical skills by being trained to search and analyse relevant information in an efficient systematical way. Therefore, I possess a strong attention for detail and have an excellent knowledge of the law.

19 Covering rules on UNCITRAL, ICC etc.

Besides my LLM, I am working as a legal recruitment consultant, where I primarily headhunt partners. Two of my main tasks are researching the market and matching candidates with firms by approaching them with the right opportunity. This role requires me to be confident and proactive, and I have to show a lot of initiative. Consequently, I have to demonstrate my communication skills, both verbally and in writing, at a high level. I have to oversee all the established relationships and work mainly with Excel to keep it organised. Thus, I possess excellent technical document management skills. The working hours are flexible and I like to be in a challenging environment. Also, in previous roles, I was required to be very communicative, managerial and organised as demonstrated in my CV. Above all, I come from a very organised house; thus, I have been brought up with these skills since I was young.

The reason why I applied for this role is that I would like to bridge the gap between theory and practice. Being in an international commercial environment is what I desire most because of its challenges, dynamics and variety. The types of cases and the opportunity to work on, for example, an £800 million claim, intrigues me. I have always liked to work in teams, and I always endeavor to be surrounded by a wide range of people. Furthermore, the firm is very reputable and known for its high standards. In 2007, I worked for a week at the office in The Hague which I really enjoyed, and I hope to become part of the London office.

Thank you for your time and I am looking forward to your response.

Yours sincerely,

Daniela Vinkeles Melchers

8.2.2 *To another law firm for a placement scheme*

Daniela Vinkeles Melchers
Address
Telephone
Email

Ms D. Thakhori
Graduate Recruitment Manager
Freshfields
Address

19 October 2019

Dear Ms Thakhori,

Application for the 2019 winter placement scheme

My name is Daniela Vinkeles Melchers, and I am writing to apply for the 2019 winter work placement. I have recently finalised my LLM in International Commercial Law at City University of London, and I completed an LLB in Law at the University of Amsterdam.

I am confident that I possess the necessary skills and drive to become a successful lawyer at Freshfields. My academic background and extracurricular activities demonstrate my keen interest to pursue a career in commercial law. Throughout my studies I have participated in various extracurricular programmes to complement my academic curriculum and strengthen my personal competences. This is best illustrated by my participation in the . . ., as well as my initiative to organise the participation of UNISCA, a Model United Nations Program. These undertakings have considerably advanced my academic curriculum, as well as strengthened my personal skills. Furthermore, during my work experience for a commercial law firm, I have demonstrated my strengths as a diligent, dependable team player, with excellent communication skills, which has further encouraged me to pursue a career as a commercial lawyer.

I am very impressed by the high calibre work, the global reach of Freshfields, as well as the outstanding reputation in all fields of law that are of particular interest to me. Furthermore, I am convinced that your unique non-rotational training system offers trainees the necessary exposure and experience to become all-round commercial lawyers.

I am positive that your award-winning work placement is an excellent opportunity to experience your inter-disciplinary training system as well as a chance for me to demonstrate my competences. I would therefore very much welcome an opportunity to discuss my application in a personal interview.

Yours sincerely,

Daniela Vinkeles Melchers

8.2.3 An email I wrote to a partner directly

Dear Mr Jones,

To attract your attention amid the many emails you receive every day, I am seizing this opportunity to apply for a speculative paralegal position.

During my LLM, I wrote essays on issues such as ICSID, UNCITRAL, ICC, BITs and umbrella clauses. Therefore, I really admire your work and would feel very honoured to have the opportunity to work for you. Moreover, I am trilingual – a native Dutch speaker, fluent in German and English. I see you and the practice group have a lot of involvement with the Dutch, so I thought my (transferable) skill set might be useful to you.

I am a high performer and an eager learner. During my other roles, I have learned to solve problems under pressure, deal with high volumes and collaborate in a team. I obtained a master's degree in law, specialising in international commercial law, and possess a profound understanding of several legal systems, including international law, common law and civil law. I have also been involved with reputable firms and had no resits for my LLM. My diverse background can contribute to innovative ideas and solutions.

I am applying for a speculative paralegal position at X because of the quality of the complex work, the partners in the International Arbitration section and the type of cases, such as *X3, etc.* In short, I would like to become amazingly skilled, just like you, and thus I directed my letter to you.

Many thanks in advance for your consideration and time. Please find attached my CV, and I look forward to hearing from you.

Warm regards,

Daniela Vinkeles Melchers